Law and Dynamic Administration

Law and Dynamic Administration

Marshall E. Dimock

PRAEGER

PRAEGER SPECIAL STUDIES • PRAEGER SCIENTIFIC

Library of Congress Cataloging in Publication Data

Dimock, Marshall Edward, 1903-
  Law and dynamic administration.

  Bibliography: p.
  1. Administrative law--United States. 2. Judicial
review of administrative acts--United States. 3. Administrative procedure--United States. I. Title.
KF5402.D56   342.73'06   80-12863
ISBN 0-03-057367-X
ISBN 0-03-057396-3 (pbk.)

Published in 1980 by Praeger Publishers
CBS Educational and Professional Publishing
A Division of CBS, Inc.
521 Fifth Avenue, New York, New York 10017 U.S.A.

© 1980 by Praeger Publishers

0123456789   145 987654321

Printed in the United States of America

PREFACE

A group of foresighted businessmen has created a nonprofit organization to study ways to reduce unnecessary litigation and time-consuming contentiousness. In the late 1970s dozens of like-minded groups sprang up to search for the causes of excessive government regulation and the means to free management for more dynamic administration. Today others are seeking to make representative government more effective, especially in its "vital" functions, such as foreign affairs and economic stabilization.

Proliferation of rules and regulations stifles dynamic management, by which I mean management in government as well as in business. Lawyers are largely responsible, but others deserve their share of credit—personnel experts, bureaucrats, and labor unions, for example. The main alliance, however, is that between business and the big law firms.

This book is an attempt to discover the underlying reasons why lawyers tend to tie up managers in knots, thus reducing competitiveness and productivity. After explaining public administrators and lawyers to one another, I try to show how they can profit the country by working in better accord.

I have received advice and encouragement from several sources; but I want to express special thanks to my wife, Gladys Ogden Dimock; to Diane Brownell, who typed my manuscript; and to some of my friends who are members of the National Academy of Public Administration. I have been studying bureaucracy and enterprise in business and government since 1932; hence the names of others to whom I am grateful will appear as my thesis develops.

Marshall E. Dimock
Scrivelsby
Bethel, Vermont
February 1980

CONTENTS

— *PART ONE* —

DOMINATION OR TEAMWORK?

— *1* —

A NEW EQUILIBRIUM

Lawyers as a class are powerful in the United States; so are business executives. But public administrators, who do substantially the same kind of work, are, in terms of clout, a faint imitation of these other two groups. Government administration is weak, considerably weaker than it was during the New Deal; the conservative reaction to the New Deal had something to do with the subsequent decline of the government's administrative effectiveness. This campaign climaxed in 1946 with the passage of the Administrative Procedure Act. First, federal administration, and following that, a large percentage of state administrations, began to judicialize, which made them progressively tentative, formalistic, and bureaucratic.[1]

There were a number of reasons for this decline; one was the possibly well-intentioned campaign of the U.S. legal profession, which already controlled Congress and the courts, to bring the administrative services also under its control. What was represented as an attempt to strengthen private rights and due process of law became, by gradual extension and in actual operation, a progressive slowing down and confusion of the administrative process. That legalistic invasion now needs to be relaxed before administration can once again become dynamic. It must be made dynamic because there are some functions of government that, if allowed to atrophy, might endanger national survival.

A key to what has been happening is the method of training lawyers. They study something called administrative law but there is

3

little of administration in it. They come out of law school with a blind spot in this area and a prejudice, instead of an understanding of how crucial good administration is. I hope here to do something about improving their understanding of administration, and at the same time encourage administrators to be less antagonistic to lawyers and the law than they are now. Administrators need freedom to become leaders;[2] lawyers need a more mature view of the government's business.

The principle of balance, which is much explored by both the physicist and the biologist, can present even more intricate problems for the student of social institutions. A case in point, which carries a heavy freight for both our economic and political institutions, is the one I propose to examine: the balance that ought to exist between judge-made law and administrative-made law. Both are a part of "the law," which is a nebulous thing but which, because it involves our Bill of Rights and property, we support with great intensity and devotion. Both the administrative and judicial branches of government originated from a common historical source and became specialized only a few centuries ago. But today they are unfortunately antagonistic toward each other.

Administration calls itself activist because its ultimate test is what it accomplishes in the way of things produced or services rendered. The law, on the other hand, and especially its judicial expression, has long prided itself on its conservatizing effect upon society. It follows precedents, and precedents that relate to a bygone age are not necessarily congruent with current requirements, such as ecology or labor relations. So though both lawyers and administrators are pledged to observe the law and although both are engaged in its execution (the legislature being the maker of the law), they have become increasingly antagonistic. As recently as 1974, for example, one of England's most respected and highest-ranking judges, Sir Leslie Scarman, expressed in his Hamlyn Lectures the opinion that if remedial steps are not taken soon, the common law will be out weighed by law originating from administration, that there would be two systems of law instead of one, and that this weakening and confusion of the constitutional certainties that have long prevailed in Great Britain might be a main cause of economic and political decline.[3]

This is no less true in the United States. In fact, I think that because the number of lawyers is so great in the United States and some of them seek employment by interfering unnecessarily with administration (usually through their professional associations) that the dangers of economic and political decay stemming from this cause may be even greater in this country than in the United Kingdom. Further, I believe that one of the reasons why both countries have been concerned with institutional decline is that in professedly trying to strengthen private rights, the legal profession and the judiciary (though in lesser degree) have unwittingly weakened the administrative activism that representative governments need quite as much as dictatorships. The result is that the inertia, lowered morale, and general debilitation of U.S. governmental institutions go a long way toward accounting for the national decline that is so often commented upon.

Although I speak of the conflict between the professional outlooks and aims of the two professions, my objective is to avoid the charge that I am taking sides one against the other. My object is to analyze the outlooks and competences of the lawyers' and the administrators' skills and, in as constructive a way as possible, suggest how a better understanding and accommodation between the two viewpoints may be secured.

My belief is that I am equally loyal to both groups, the reason being that I am a protégé of two of the greatest legal students this country has produced: W. W. Willoughby in constitutional law, and Frank J. Goodnow, who is universally acknowledged as the father of administrative law in the United States. For many years, both at UCLA and later at the University of Chicago, I taught courses on constitutional and administrative law. Equally, again beginning with the Chicago period, I have written extensively on public administration and have been a practitioner of it, especially at the federal level and for the United Nations, for several consecutive years of my life. If in this dual experience I have any professional bias (and, like everyone else, I am sure I do in varying degree) it is in the direction of recognizing the necessities of the line or program manager. In the U.S. economic system he is the most admired person of all—self-made, a rugged individualist, the person who turns out all the goods and services that characterize the consumer civilization.

However, his counterpart, the bureau chief in government, gains nothing but disapproval. Increasingly, since the New Deal period of the 1930s, he has become the forgotten man. He is called a bureaucrat and as such is charged with creating rules and red tape that prove obnoxious to almost everyone; but in reality his reputation is undeserved. In fact much of this red tape is imposed upon him. The government executive would like to be freer than he is, but increasingly since about 1946 he has been tied up in bureaucratic rules at all points in his professional life, from the making of the law he is expected to administer, through the procedures he is required to follow (often against his better judgment), to the decisions he is required to make in the course of his work.

As he has become more rule ridden and required to stress procedure and not substance (which is contrary to his natural instinct), he becomes in effect a glorified clerk, a colorless routineer, a pusher of papers, in short, impotent. He is reduced to playing games instead of keeping his eyes focused on production. Needing discretion and flexibility if he is really to become activist, he discovers that his province is increasingly invaded by the lawyers, who in their organized capacity exercise the real power. The United States has reached the point in its national life that a distinguished French jurist, Edouard Lambert of the University of Lyon, called the government of lawyers and judges.

The lawyers alone, of course, cannot be blamed for the increasing ineffectuality of government at the federal level. The civil service mentality is a part of it. Congress is often distressingly slow to act in periods of national emergency, such as the energy crunch, and is even slower about improving its own internal organization and performance. Teamwork between the president and Congress is nowhere near as good as it should be if vitality and responsibility are to be wedded. The court system and the administration of justice have made some notable improvements in recent years, but there is still much congestion of dockets and failure to discover better alternative ways of handling cases and controversies. Justice is costly, slow, and in need of additional improvement. Underlying all this institutional lethargy, however, and explaining why it is allowed to continue, is a citizen attitude of hostility and lack of comprehension of why government is important and what its priorities and necessities are.

Organized business and labor, combined with the antigovernment campaigns of powerful pressure groups such as the American Medical Association and the American Bar Association, have had much to do with the distrustful state of citizen opinion. But in this campaign the lawyers, both within and outside government, have spearheaded the movement. One of the most significant achievements of the lawyers' success, partly because they are so numerous, is the weakening, sometimes unwittingly, of public administration as a vital force.

The balances that are needed are of several kinds, but all are related. The first and basic one, because it explains the temper and spirit of the voters, is a better equilibrium between the concepts of private and public interest. Lawyers, more than any other class, need this "return to religion" because they were once, with the clergy, the main champions of the public interest, but they are now almost wholly dedicated to making money. In this earlier period law was thought to be derived from morality, being a branch of it. So greatly has the situation changed that even textbook writers usually start their treatises with the assertion that private law is the exclusive preserve of the lawyer and winning cases is the test of his effectiveness. For decades little was heard about ethics and self-government of the legal profession, but since Watergate there has begun to be a revived interest in these questions.

The second major reconciliation that would help to restore equilibrium is a clearer appreciation of what is meant by the nebulous term, "the law," and what its metes and bounds are. Without this it is difficult, if not impossible, to work out a division of labor that avoids the conflicts and stalemates that now prevail. Fortunately, in the last few years there has been a considerable resurgence of interest in the philosophy of the law and this is a source of great encouragement. This clarification bears directly on the present study. If law is universal fairness, then everyone has a part in contributing to these values. The lawyer and the administrator would be considered equal, although each has a different set of skills and a difference in outlook concerning role. To take a different illustration, if law is an adjustment of rights and duties to the changed circumstances of national life— such things as environment and labor relations—then as of old the administrator should be the activist and the judge the reviewer of fairness and of consistency with constitutional principles. Or take the moral dimension again: if law derives from morality and both the law and the courts are part of the governmental system (as clearly they are), the only way justice can be kept moral and ethical is to assure that the entire government, including the legislative and executive branches of the political state, partake of the same qualities.

The third and ultimately the most important balance that needs restoring, however, is that that has to do with the survival of what in the United States is called "free" institutions. By this is usually meant the individual competitive system and the Constitution based upon the idea of popular sovereignty. The thesis of this book is that if government becomes too impotent both are likely to suffer and in the long run will disappear. A further thesis is that the weakest part of the U.S. system at present is the administration of the law, or what is sometimes called the executive side of government. It is weak because it does not accomplish enough. It fails to accomplish more because it is not allowed to operate with the clear mandate, the autonomy, and the flexibility and discretion that universal experience with executive work proves are necessary. Too little is achieved from too large an expenditure of money. Hence the country's problems accumulate, the people become dissatisfied and pessimistic, and the decline of institutions is the result.

There are many ways of reversing the trend. The one to be considered here is a better definition of skills and teamwork, in the public interest, of the legal profession and the profession of public administration. This takes the following form: What are the principles of administrative law and of public administration that are consonant? How can the two fields of knowledge be reconciled as to their differences of outlook and doctrine so as to become more effective partners?

The interconnection of administrative law and public administration raises some questions that are of the greatest importance to the individual enterprise system and to political and economic theory. These questions are especially timely in the United States at this juncture in its national life, as many seek to make both the economy and the government more effective in accomplishing their respective tasks.

The central problem arising from this nexus of law and administration is this: how to make government more responsible to standards that take the form of law as enforced by the courts, and in so doing afford proper protection to individual and economic rights, while at the same time making the performance of government more efficient and enterprising, thus assuring the continued vitality of both the private enterprise system and representative government. If this reconciliation fails, the alternative ultimately would become some form of socialism in which the public sector would do relatively more than now, while the private sector had less autonomy and hence less freedom.

This reconciliation has been insufficiently emphasized in recent U.S. scholarship. Prior to the New Deal and its aftermath the situation was different. The earliest scholars, such as Frank J. Goodnow, deliberately set out to interrelate the law and the practical side of administration, realizing that either subject, in splendid isolation, afforded little assurance that the best elements of both fields could succeed unless the matrices represented by administrative law and practical management were closely and successfully integrated.

The reasons that the two subjects have become autarchical since the late 1930s and early 1940s are readily discernible. The main reason is that although political science's influence, stressing fundamental political theory, succeeded in placing the relationship in wider perspective during the formative period from 1890 to the outbreak of

World War II, after that time the law schools and the legal scholars began to exercise a dominant influence. Second, due to the attempt in political science to release the subject from the bondage of the lawyers (Charles A. Beard's phrase) and the legal mind, political scientists unwittingly tended to neglect law as a subject in their desire to eliminate the parochial attitudes they were protesting against. Simultaneously, for such is the nature of overspecialization, the law school approach became that of stressing private law and neglecting public law, the assumption apparently being that private law represents the majesty of the law as an abstract proposition, because there is more symmetry and less diversity in the myth of a unified system of law than in the coalescence of the two elements that earlier scholars stressed and that tied both subjects closely to fundamental political theory. In his later writings, Roscoe Pound was one of those who exercised a notable influence in bringing about this transformation. Another, more closely related to the field of administrative law, was Ernst Freund of the University of Chicago. Freund started out as a political scientist, but in the course of his development he became the champion of the more restricted view of administrative law as concerned primarily, or almost wholly, with private law.

The separation of the two fields was accentuated by the emergence in the 1930s of the rapidly growing profession of public administration,* which emphasized the techniques of production and getting things done, in the meantime leaving the development of administrative law largely to the law schools and their legal scholars.

An important third factor was ideological. In the reaction against the burgeoning of governmental activity stemming from the New Deal—a reaction that Aristotle safely could have predicted—powerful pressure groups moved into the arena and developed the view that

---

* A word about the meaning of terms: "public administration" is both an academic subject and a governmental vocation, the largest of all. When I use the term in these two senses I shall try to make clear which I intend. As an academic subject, public administration (in the United States) has long been a subdivision within the parent field of political science (politics, government). Beginning about 1938, however, public administration became so much emphasized and the direction in which political science was going (toward value-free analysis) was so uncongenial to academic public administrators that it has achieved a degree of academic independence, with separate schools and separate degrees in a growing number of cases. Professionally, both groups, the academics and the practitioners, are organized into two overall professional associations: the American Society for Public Administration and the National Academy of Public Administration. There also are a score of specialized professional associations, such as the International City Managers Association. When I use "political science" or "public administration" I shall attempt to keep these distinctions clear.

administrative law is mainly concerned with protecting private rights. This in effect relegated managerial considerations to the public administration profession as Freund already had decided to do.

The abdication of political science and the growing influence of the legal profession took the form of the judicialization of the administrative process. Its main manifestations were the Walter-Logan Bill of 1938, which was vetoed, and the administrative procedure acts, both federal and state, which were enacted shortly after the Report of the Attorney-General's Committee on Administrative Procedure in 1941, the federal act dating from 1946. Two consequences of this successful campaign tended to dilute and make less effective the work of government managers. The first was to make the lawyer and his way of looking at life gradually more dominant over the public administrator, whose duty is to stress production and to give full effect to laws on the statute books. The second was to fracture the unity and coalescence of factors needed to assure the efficient production of governmental goods and services. This need to public as well as private management has been set forth convincingly in Peter Drucker's book, *Management: Tasks, Responsibilities, Practices* (1973), but the need for autonomy and a certain degree of freedom of management was appreciated long before this. As V. M. Barnett, Jr. said in his "Judicialization of the Administrative Process" in *Public Administrative Review* (Spring 1948), judicialization has a creeping, insidious character to it that is not apparent all at once.

The present-day problem, then, is to synthesize legal and managerial thinking in some form of effective unity in order to achieve the best of both worlds, and in so doing strengthen the chances that the private enterprise system and popularly controlled government will be able to withstand the challenge of class-controlled socialisms. Government must be made responsive and efficient as well as accountable and limited by the law. Governments are run by people as well as by legal rules. Law is not a mystical entity, a floating omnipresence in the sky; it is the rules that both courts and managers follow. It is the old problem of an effective division of labor, not the complete dominance of one or the other.

The reconciliation needed today is by no means a simple matter. Conceits are involved on both sides. If it were simply a matter of logic and recombining common elements in law and management, the exercise would be taxing, but it would be by no means unworkable. What complicates the problem is the human element. Both the lawyers and the managers are fiercely attached to the omniscience of their respective crafts.

The lawyers argue that law is a universal—it has a separate

existence based upon custom, precedent, and first principles. Second, it is assumed that law is rules, and that where there are not rules there is license. Consequently, management is also a matter of rules. The more rules there are, say the lawyers, the more justice there will be, because discretion will be obviated, and discretion is the antithesis of rule. From these assumptions it follows that management is ministerial, that is, performing more or less by rote the duties laid down in the rules. Those who make the rules are superior and dominant, while those who carry out assigned tasks are the equivalent of bookkeepers or anyone who performs carefully circumscribed tasks. Small wonder, then, that on the basis of this logic the lawyer should be dominant and the manager subordinate. Besides, the United States has more lawyers than other countries, and therefore jobs must be made for lawyers or the continual expansion of legal manpower will be jeopardized.

The assumptions of the management craft, although equally cabined and confined, run pretty much to the opposite conclusions. Management is law in action. The law is a source but not the vehicle. The vehicle is the integrative and entrepreneurial mind of the manager that establishes and defines goals and then martials all the elements needed, such as organization, personnel, finance, and technique, to produce social and individual benefits that outweigh the total costs of production. Hence, instead of the manager being a bureaucratic automaton, this professional view holds that the manager is the key person in the whole complex of skills. Law and lawyers, they say, are only one element and not necessarily the most important. Law is conservatizing, management is enterprising. If managers did nothing but follow rules, nothing of major consequence would ever be accomplished in meeting society's needs. Hence to the extent that lawyers act like superior persons, they are to be either shunted aside or treated with suspicion and veiled contempt. In effect, they become the enemy, the enemy of accomplishment. Thus in both cases arrogance is met with an opposing arrogance. The contentions that occur in the marketplace, the legislative chamber, and the courtroom are transposed into the administrative process, with each side vying for power.

The problem is exacerbated because of differing psychological outlooks. The manager prides himself on being an integrator, for this is his stock-in-trade. He has a skill that very few human beings possess to a marked degree. The lawyer, on the other hand, is trained to be contentious, always looking for lacunae in the interpretation of words and phrases that will permit his side to win a victory, irrespective of its immediate effect upon standards of abstract justice or the interests of society in survival and group well-being. In short, the manager measures his success by goods and services, the lawyer by winning a case. This problem is made more acute because most lawyers know little or nothing about management philosophy and technique. Hence when they become managers, as many do because of the calculus of supply and demand, the lawyer who becomes successful as a manager needs to change one set of assumptions for another set, and in so doing changes his outlook on life and even his whole personality. Lawyers are sticklers for detail, managers see whole systems and the role of enterprise and personality influence.

This difference of orientation comes to focus on the central problem of discretion. Without a sufficient discretion to fix targets, develop a strategy, and integrate the parts of a vast administrative scheme, the manager cannot achieve significant successes. Accordingly, it is a short step to contend, as many managers do, that the manager is the servant of society as a whole and the legal profession is the servant of vested interests. There is no such thing as the law in the abstract. It is a matter of power brokerage in which the claims of society and the special interests forever vie with each other. Hence the central problem becomes one and the same as that of political philosophy's central concern: how to reconcile the just claims of the society as a whole and the equally just claims of individuals who seek to protect their own rights and interests.

The obvious solution to this conflict of rival skill groups is to incorporate more managerial thinking into administrative law and more administrative law, in the sense of fairness and due process, into the preparation of managers. The need is undoubtedly greater in the case of those who become government managers than in the case of those who serve corporations and the private sector, but the latter group also should be exposed to this admixing of factors if the private enterprise system and the government are to work together effectively for the good of the entire citizenry.

The first step in seeking this needed reconciliation is to regain one's sense of historical evolution, which is the province of jurisprudence and legal ethics. W. F. Willoughby has explained this interdependence about as clearly as any U.S. scholar ever has. In his trilogy *Principles of Judicial Administration*, *Principles of Legislative Organization and Administration*, and *Principles of Public Administration*, Willoughby pointed out what legal scholars have long known but many have forgotten in recent years. The legislature makes the policy, while the administrators and the judiciary equally have the responsibility for giving it practical effect in the form of enforcement. Historically, there was no formal division into administration and adjudication as separate and distinct processes and institutions because adjudication initially grew out of administration. Accordingly, as Willoughby convincingly points out, the members of both specialized crafts have their appointed role in shaping and developing the law once it has been tailored by the legislature and in supplying rules and decision-making processes in making law applicable to the particular case and controversy. In the light of the law, therefore, both the manager and lawyer-judge have an equal concern with an interest in the law, whether it be constitutional, common law, statutory, or administrative. Administrative law is best described as the law in action.

Moreover, as society has become more organized and complex and as government has entered more and more fields of common concern, what is described as administrative law becomes immensely large and complex. It is not merely the so-called regulatory aspects of government activity—although in late years there are those who would confine it to that—but it is also what every agency of government does in lesser or greater degree when officials exercise their rule-making and deciding powers as inevitable consequences of the general objectives and policies laid down by legislative bodies. Here again, another difference arises in the outlook of managers and judges. The manager sees this subprocess as part of a much greater process in which integration, drive, planning, and skill are needed. The lawyer and judge, on the other hand, because of professional predisposition, tend to look upon rules and decisions as discrete, meaning that they apply only to a given case or controversy affecting private versus public interest. The distinction is a proper and necessary one, for it is an integral part of the checks and balances that any popular government must needs respect if liberty and justice are to be respected in every case. But each aspect of the process clearly benefits when all parties to disputes—managers, lawyers, and the judges—are aware of the systemic interest as well as the individual interest involved in the particular case.

In studying and teaching administrative law, the vastness of the subject quite understandably has resulted in stressing process more than substance. For in the time available to teaching institutions, it would be quite impossible to teach in one course all the intricacies of all subjects where the government is a party. Hence, as is presently the case in the United States, the practical solution is to teach the common elements and philosophies of the administrative process and leave to more specialized courses such as tax law, labor law, consumer law, and all the rest, the deeper probings into these substantive fields.

Although this need to circumscribe the focus of teaching in administrative law and public administration on common elements exists, it is also the counsel of wisdom to include equal elements of managerial and legal philosophy in the main course on administrative law if society's legitimate needs are to be respected. Managers should be trained to respect and understand the law, and equally lawyers should be trained to understand and respect the special skills and outlooks found in the dedicated manager. For otherwise, with the best of intentions, the inevitable result of a truncated focus and philosophy would be to invite the weakening of institutions called attention to earlier.

NOTES

1. By 1978 there were no less than 1,000 administrative law judges working in 28 federal agencies. The budgeted cost of regulation to the federal government was $3 billion, and to the private sector ranged from $16 billion to $130 billion. *Administrative Law Process: Better Management is Needed*, Report of the Comptroller General to Congress, May 15, 1978.

2. See my article, "Revitalized Program Management," *Public Administration Review* 38 (May-June 1978): 199-204.

3. Sir Leslie Scarman, *English Law—The New Dimension*, the Hamlyn Lectures, Twenty-Sixth Series (London: Stevens & Sons, 1974), parts VI and VII.

— 2 —

SOME COMMON FALLACIES REGARDING ADMINISTRATION

In the long history of the political state, administration became one of the oldest and most respected professions. This is because most early governments were monarchies, and the king's most trusted lieutenants became heads of departments and were chosen not only for their loyalty but also for their ability to achieve state purposes. This story has been told in a number of places, but for convenient reference, I would refer to the following studies: Albert Lepawsky, *Administration: The Art and Science of Organization and Management* (1949); Brian Chapman, *The Profession of Government* (1959); Marver Bernstein, *The Job of the Federal Executive* (1958); and Corson and Paul, *Men Near the Top* (1966). In the Western world the earliest examples of professionalized public administration occurred in Rome and in those countries that were most directly affected by its law and culture, namely, France, Spain, and Germany.

Even in the United States, where government did not become large and influential until the advent of the New Deal in the 1930s, the administrative side now employs 95 percent of the government's employees, spends most of its revenues, and is the so-called delivery system for goods and services that the citizen enjoys. With well over two million administrators in the federal government alone and four or five times that many employed by state and local governments, U.S. governments administer presently about one-third of the gross national product; in Great Britain, the Scandinavian countries, and other representative governments the percentage is even higher. It stands to reason that so many employees, working in scores of agencies in the federal government alone, need a great deal of leadership and knowledge of managerial skills if government is to be an efficient and dynamic force instead of a dead weight or a positive liability.

Because of the antigovernment bias that has long existed in the United States and that is inculcated by organized interests seeking to be left alone, a double standard exists in thinking about the role of executives and managers in the life of the nation. Everyone takes it for granted that if a large corporation like American Telephone is efficiently managed and commands public respect, it is because its management is principled and efficient. This is a rational view and quite sound. Similarly, as Peter Drucker clearly establishes in his magnum opus, *Management: Tasks, Responsibilities, Practices* (1973), the United States' phenomenal production, high living standard, and record of enterprising achievement is due largely, though not exclusively, to the high level of managerial acumen it has developed in the private sector. This is seen most clearly when the United States is compared to countries where these skills have not yet been developed or when a hard look is taken at countries where economic and institutional decline are occurring. Managerial skill is a measurable variable; it can be lost as well as enhanced. Hence when some lawyers, out of sheer ignorance, denigrate administration and its professionals, which some of them do in order to enhance their own power and authority, they demonstrate an ignorance of history and institutional growth and decay.

The principle that explains the need for leadership in large governments (as in the private sector) may be stated as follows: the more subdivided and specialized an organization becomes and the more rules and procedures it is expected to follow, the more bureaucratic it becomes and consequently the more leadership it requires if internal inertia is to be activated into cooperative accomplishment. Further, it needs motivated employees, with interest in their work and some challenge in the form of flexibility and discretion if they are to put forth their best efforts. Organizations of humans that are treated like machines do not produce like machines. Often they do not produce at all. At best they produce at a low level of efficiency. When crises arise, as invariably they do, the ability to respond is suspect or nonexistent. Therefore the cost of impotent organizations is human and monetary waste, failure to accomplish national objectives, and a weakening of the country's competitive position in the world. A good executive is at least as valuable as a wise lawmaker or a virtuous judge. When an executive fails, the public sickens of government and loses its morale. The government simply appoints more people, where fewer are needed, and in consequence matters rapidly become worse. When lawyers unwittingly undermine good administration they undermine themselves, because the free enterprise system and free government cannot survive without effective government executives.

A convincingly accurate reason for the antigovernment bias on the part of many intelligent U.S. citizens is based upon principle. It is that good constitutions incorporate the principle of limited government. Failing to write the limitations into the constitution, the government, in time, may abuse people's rights, attempt to do too much, or both. It is a sound instinct and an equally sound standard. But there are two balancing principles that should be enunciated at the same time, as in physics. The first is that a government should do as well as possible those things that are expressly provided for in the constitution, or, if this is not done, the people may in time turn against the constitution and also its bill of rights. The second is that if those who swear to uphold the constitution attempt through their pressure groups or other forms of conspiracy and influence to undermine the sovereign will as expressed in legislation by attempting to make its administration unworkable, they are, in effect, undermining the spirit of the law and hence bring law and constitutions into disrespect. In other words, there is no principle of logic or of law that can sustain the contention that the means justifies the end. This takes the form of people's saying that the only way to secure limited government is deliberately to make administration inefficient. People who really believe this, and act accordingly, invite disaster. The best place for a conservative or an anarchist to fight is in the open.

There is another thing that some lawyers, in their zeal to be Washington lawyers, do not seem to appreciate. A government of pressure groups is not a government of laws. If one wants constitutional government one should work through it, not around it. Again the reason is that to create disrespect for government causes equal disrespect for law and lawyers. True, Congress needs to be reformed. Administration could be vastly improved and in most respects was better during the New Deal and World War II than it has been since. But the constitutional way to attack these problems is at the source, by improving the institutions themselves, not by using backdoor stealth and hamstringing the administrative process. Lawyers should be patriots and put the public interest on a pedestal, or they should not be lawyers at all. As H.G. Wells suggested in *The Work, Wealth and Happiness of Mankind*, the lawyer's or administrator's oath should mean as much to the individual as the physician's or the priest's. Law at one time can not mean principle and at another privilege and double-dealing.

A major difficulty with the lawyer mentality is that too often the lawyers want to reduce all individual and group behavior to rules. In so doing they strike at the very essence of effective administrative performance. Administration is not adjudication. It is the use of intelligence, contrivance, and teamwork begetting unity and effectiveness, which empirically and by experimentation translates social aspiration into tangible goods and services. The lawyer and judge *find* the law, the administrator *applies* it. Administrators need infinitely more discretion than judges, and when this discretion is withheld by rules that are not of their own making and that militate against empirical problem solving, administration becomes impotent and the people suffer.

President Carter's reorganizer for personnel management, Alan Campbell, has described the difficulty in these words:

> Some have argued that to solve the problems associated with federal personnel management would require the addition of even more rules and regulations. One could envision a system in which every action would have a check and balance, and every decision a multi-level review. This might eradicate abuse, but it would also thwart productivity. A balance needs to be struck between the freedom necessary to service the public's needs and the oversight required to protect the system's integrity.[1]

The time that Campbell envisages has already arrived, as he makes clear in some of the illustrations adduced in his article. The law should be inside administration, the judge as a reserve remedy should remain outside it. To fully judicialize administration is to kill it.

There is a variation of the judicialization theme that is equally wrongheaded. C. H. Sisson, writing in a book called *The Spirit of British Administration* (1959), contends that the administrator's role is "to maintain the unity of the political group." *What* political group? Anyone that happens to be in power? If that were all that is expected of the administrator, what would happen to his respect for the law and the constitution, or even his self-respect? The administrator is not a chameleon. He is paid to think and contrive. He should seek and recommend solutions to problems in which he is expert, if for no other reason than to maintain his own integrity. Sisson goes so far as to say, "He should not be a man of ideas; his distinguishing quality should be rather a certain freedom from ideas," and "Officials are men, who, in the last desperation, exhibit a scruple."[2]

If this portrait of an executive were taken seriously, there is no better formula for assuring the demise of free institutions. Administrators and judges alike, as suggested by Justice Scarman, are, or should be, activists seeking to help society solve its problems of growth and change. Desperation, indeed! If administrators made known their scruples only when things become desperate, one might expect this state of desperation to become chronic. The better view, the one holding that administrators need principles and strong motivation to guide them, is found in a recent book based upon the lives of administrators like Haldane, Stamp, and Beveridge, *The British Philosophy of Administration* (1978), by Rosamund Thomas.

Turning now to the legal profession's view of administration, the first thing to note is that lack of knowledge of what administration is all about is frequently a more significant reason for antagonistic attitudes toward public administration than participation in pressure group activity and propaganda as mentioned earlier. Putting it another way, the Washington law firm and its counterpart at state capitols unquestionably explain much of the attempt to judicialize the whole of the administrative process (irrespective of what their motivation may be), but what is more significant is that since about 1938 lawyers and future judges have been brought up on a narrow and distorted view of administration. Administration, per se, has not been offered in the law school curriculum, although it should be in connection with either legal history and jurisprudence or administrative law. Second, courses on administrative law, with a few exceptions to be noted later, present a truncated, distorted, prejudiced view of administration. Instead of teaching public law—that is, the organization and administration of the government and the respective rights of the government and the citizen to exercise certain powers and legal restraints and remedies—the course is taught from the standpoint of private law exclusively, which immediately does two things: creates a bias and makes the student think that all administrators are "queer," if not pathological. It is as if in a medical school anatomy were not taught before taking up pathology.

An example of this is the latest book of Bernard Schwartz, one of the most prolific writers on administrative law this country has produced and a very good scholar. His 1976 book, entitled *Administrative Law*, starts out by making it explicitly clear that the course is not a course that deals with public administration; second, it does not deal with the substantive law made by administrative agencies; third, it does not deal with substantive law at all; fourth, it deals exclusively with procedure; and fifth, it is concerned primarily with the judicial process inside regulatory agencies. As a final caveat, Schwartz states that administrative law is not concerned with all administrative agencies but only those that affect private rights.[3] Ours, says Schwartz, is a "lawyer-dominated society" (p. 292), and administration, in comparison, sounds like a caricature. Starting with the thesis, "Effective administration of schemes of regulation or social service presupposes a concentration of functions foreign to the judicial process" (p. 10), he presents this picture of how public administration operates:

> The position of the department head is quite different [from regulatory tribunals]. He is usually a politician and cannot be expected to have too great a knowledge of, or even interest in, administration. The department he heads is a huge, conglomerate mass; the specific administrative task is a small part of his activities. The Secretary cannot hope to have more than a superficial knowledge of these activities. The consequence is extensive subdelegation; decisions rendered in the name of the Secretary have actually been made by some subordinate official (p. 15).

His picture makes one shudder. There is no question about it: the departments—lock, stock, and barrel—should be turned over to the judiciary to run.

It is easy to pass Schwartz's dicta off as merely the prejudices of a conservative, but it really is not that. Most conservatives have a natural respect for good administration because they pride themselves on being practical. The explanation for Schwartz's belief lies elsewhere.

The early development of U.S. administrative law began educationally during the last quarter of the nineteenth century and was almost entirely the work of political scientists, or political scientists turned law school faculty. It included such names as Frank J. Goodnow, John Dickinson, Ernst Freund, John Fairlie, Edward S. Corwin, Oliver Field, Robert Cushman, and Charles Grove Haines. Many of these men, like Goodnow, studied in Europe and literally imported administrative law from the continent, where it had been a dominant influence for at least 100 years. So numerous were the political science professors of administrative law and so few the law school teachers that it is not too much to say that administrative law grew out of political science courses (and they a branch of philosophy) until around 1940. Then the balance turned. The law schools took over this course, for the most part, and the number of administrative law professors in political science became very few indeed. Schwartz prefers to overlook all this, asserting instead that administrative law did not commence in the United States until fairly late in the twentieth century.

It was around 1940 that the field began to be narrowed as to scope. Gradually it stopped being public law and became private law. At the same time it confined its attention almost exclusively to procedures and the decision function in administration. With that foothold established, it has spread its influence so persistently that it now dominates public administration in most fields, especially at the federal level, and increasingly at the state level as well. The impetus to the rapid judicialization of administration occurred with the passage of the Administrative Procedure Act of 1946, sponsored by the American Bar Association and using the *Morgan* decisions of the U.S. Supreme Court as the launching pad. *Morgan* had to do with administrative procedure. This was the clue: all of public administration should be viewed as procedure, and the key to procedure, of course, is rules. So there began in 1940 a drive to convert public administration into rules, procedures, and adjudication, a conversion, which if it were to succeed, would completely bastardize a field essential to national survival.

Another law school professor of administrative law, Walter Gellhorn of Columbia University, prophetically saw what was likely to happen because he, in the university where Goodnow first established administrative law, was in the political science tradition (Columbia's Department of Public Law and Jurisprudence is the oldest department of political science in the United States today). In Gellhorn's *Administrative Law: Cases and Comments* (1940), the author, by way of introduction, starts with a quote demonstrating the deep bias that already existed in 1940 toward the administrative branch of government, saying "there is no doubt that many lawyers and judges regard administrative agencies and their staffs with suspicion if not active enmity" (p. 2). Then, turning to the attacks on New Deal agencies commenced by the American Bar Association and leading to the Walter-Logan Bill of 1938, which was vetoed, and followed thereafter by the Administrative Procedure Act of 1946, Gellhorn observes, "opponents of administrative power are not concerned at bottom by the methods and procedures of administrative agencies, but are in fact hostile to the policies which they have been appointed to further" (p. 5). These, he says, are "'untempered' attacks" (p. 8). Then he calls attention to the almost complete neglect in law school administrative law courses of the substantive (policy, administrative) aspects of the subject (p. 9). He concludes by suggesting that the issue of administrative efficiency (which is what the administrator must be interested in if his program is to succeed) "transcends in importance all problems of administrative justice" (p. 32).

It is this balancing of factors, this realistic regard for the realities of the public administration field, that is the concern of this study. This, and nothing more, for all individuals, including lawyers and judges in their private capacities, are rightly concerned with the policies adopted by legislatures. But when they permit their scruples to color their interpretation of what administration needs to accomplish in a representative government, they are untrue to the tradition of objective scholarship and are using their private thirsts for power to subvert the form of government they are pledged to uphold.

NOTES

1. Alan K. Campbell, "Civil Service Reform: A New Commitment," *Public Administration Review* 38 (March-April 1978): 103.
2. C. H. Sisson, *The Spirit of British Administration* (New York: Frederick A. Praeger, 1959), pp. 22-24.
3. Bernard Schwartz, *Administrative Law* (Boston: Little, Brown, 1976), pp. 3-4. Even his definition reveals a bias: "administrative law is that branch of the law which *controls* the administrative operations of government" p. 1. What an invitation that is to lawyer domination!

— 3 —

A MORE REALISTIC VIEW OF
THE ADMINISTRATOR'S ROLE

The ability to synthesize diverse elements is the essential that above all others distinguishes the successful administrator. If in the vocabulary of organization he is called an executive, he will have a higher level of responsibility for setting policy and making more strategic decisions than one who is called a manager. If he is a so-called line or production manager he will need to know more than others about the technology and lore of his craft or profession. Whether it is telephones or apprehending criminals, his kind of knowledge needs to be applied every day. But whether one chooses to use the term "executive" or "manager," anyone who synthesizes a body of knowledge, an organization and its people, and who needs to bring together both the know-how and people factors into some kind of measurable production, may be called an administrator. The use of these three terms differs from corporations to governments, and from country to country, but the semantics are not as important as the function, which is to unify a large number of factors in order to achieve a blend of quantity, quality, and motivation for some part of the economy, whether it is called private, public, or something in between.

There are a number of terms that are employed to describe the synthesis. The main ones are blend, mix, integration, unity, cohesiveness, autonomy, teamwork, drive. The terms employed by the lawyer, namely, "process" or "procedure," are looked upon by the administrator with suspicion because they suggest routine and habit, which require little or no thinking and contrivance, whereas the administrator's necessity, in order to be effective, is strategy and contrivance, both of which require flexibility and discretion. This is especially true in the people part of an assignment, because if they are not motivated they will not perform as a team.

Life is full of analogies and to mention some of them may enable one to see the administrator's cardinal task a bit more clearly. In developing atomic energy, the laser, or the computer—in fact, any technological product that is much discussed today—the physicist with his research into general principles, and the engineer with his knowledge of technology, need to work together to achieve an operable, relevant, salable product that enters into production. Other skills are involved as well, but the necessity of blending these two is sufficient to make the point.

Similarly, when an orchestra conductor produces for consumer satisfaction one of Beethoven's or Mozart's symphonies, it is essential that each musician do what is expected at the right time and with fidelity and feeling if the total impact on the audience is going to be sufficient to draw sustained applause. Or, to take another illustration, if the surgeon is to succeed in a delicate operation, it is essential that the laboratories give the correct diagnosis, the anesthetist perform properly, and the team of assisting surgeons and nurses provide their skilled, experienced roles at the right time and with the right effect, because the failure of any one might result in the patient's death or deformity. It is no different in the courtroom: the judge, the attorneys, the jury, and the court administrators need to produce a balanced result; if by allowing one to dominate the proceedings and the others to be neglected, the proceedings become unbalanced and subject to just complaint.

Now that what is central and distinctive in the administrator's role in society has been suggested, it is equally important to mention those respects in which his strategy of production resembles that of the lawyer-judge. The administrator customarily does the same things a law school student does in reporting on a case in the classroom. He considers: How did the case arise? What is the problem? What are the issues? What are the alternative solutions? What is the just decision? What is the reasoning?

But the administrator must do a great deal more than this. What is the policy he wants to adopt for the long haul? Second, will this decision help or hinder the long-run policies that produce the objectives he ought to keep in mind? Hence the focus is not solely or even mainly on the immediate decision but on the effect of that decision upon a number of factors that cannot be overlooked: the reputation of the firm or the government agency; the effect upon survival; the resulting impact upon the entire staff; the reaction of organized labor; the possible ramifications upon other agencies of the government, such as Congress or the courts; the political effect, because administration is an integral part of policy and is not separable; the reaction of the interest groups that are most closely identified with the program; the influence upon general public opinion; the reaction of the press and the other media of information and public opinion; and finally, the effect upon the law being administered. In addition, the administrator asks some of the same questions the judge does. Is it in accord with the Constitution and the precedents? Is it fair? Will it promote or deter litigation because of fuzziness and uncertainty? Will it add to people's respect for the law or do the opposite?

Despite these few similarities, however, it will be seen that there are so many respects in which the administrator's perspective differs from that of the judge that the two situations are not comparable. The administrator deliberately takes the long view, the political stance, the policy approach as contrasted to rule making. He needs to be sensitive to public opinion as found in employees, labor, customers, the press, and other government agencies—the list is so long that sometimes it seems to include the entire political economy.

In other words, the administrator has far more variables to consider than the judge or the lawyer; he has a more difficult job therefore synthesizing all these factors and weighing each against the others. The law and the individual decision are important, but they are merely one factor amongst many that seem equally as important. Finally, the greatest difference of all—will it work? The administrator's only payoff is results: production, hitting his target, consumer satisfaction. Not so the judge. Although marginally interested in enforceability, this is not the judge's main responsibility. Someone else, an administrative official, will have to supply the enforcement because that is outside the judge's job description. All a judge does is decide on the sanctions, which is quite a different matter than the step-by-step challenge of spelling out the stages and strategies involved in administration.

To the judge or the lawyer, the decision is everything. To the administrator the decision in each case is one among many essential factors in the flow of work. It is something to be taken in stride because it bears importantly on overall effectiveness, but it is not the end and objective of his existence.

Now one comes to the crux of the matter. What happens if in effect the decision function is removed from the administrators and immediate responsibility given to someone else? The inevitable conclusion already has been suggested: the administrator's whole ability to synthesize all elements and to direct the flow of work is jeopardized. No longer is there a unified enterprise. An overall program and strategy cannot be developed. Instead of being on top of the job—an essential feeling if he is to succeed—the administrator feels like a captive of a conquered province. He becomes confused and dispirited because instead of having a unified responsibility for program management, he cannot possibly develop a head of steam if decision-making is excised by legislative mandate and entrusted to internal administrative judges whom he does not appoint or even fully control.

The same thing is true about rules and procedures. The administrator operates on the basis of policy and sublegislation, not rules. An excessive number of rules interferes with his strategy and whole outlook. He prides himself on getting results by avoiding rules and instead motivating employees to do their jobs without tying them up in knots. Rules mean paperwork. Paperwork means a deadening bureaucracy. A rule is a negative thing. A policy is a positive thing. The administrator is therefore prepared to fight for his policy jurisdiction and resist to the death those who attempt to tie him up in lilliputian knots called rules.

To summarize the argument to this point: under his overall mandate, the administrator decides what his objectives and policies are; how his authority is to be parceled out to everyone in the organization; how the organization is going to be used for communication and coordination; how the whole thing is going to be smoothly and efficiently coordinated to give it incentive and assure that targets are being hit on schedule; and how the work may be evaluated constantly to see that it lives up to expectations and to see how it can be improved. Then he spends a lot of time selling it to all parties of interest, commencing with his own employees. In short, administration is dynamic. Law and adjudication are too static except as guideposts on the road to program planning of objectives.

Although the essence and spirit of administration has been described, it also should be appreciated (and this will come as no surprise) that there are considerable variations in the nature of work done in the government or in any other area of a nation's life. Manufacturing steel differs considerably from selling ladies' lingerie. Or, in the public sector, building roads involves quite a different combination of factors than awarding contracts to universities for basic scientific research. However, one must not make the mistake of overemphasizing these differences. The need for synthesis is a universal. So also is the necessity of avoiding the dangers of splintering unified management by mistakenly attempting to remove from the heart of administration the policy and deciding functions and turning them over to someone else.

It used to be argued, before corporations learned how wrong they can be, that industries that are essentially engineering—like steel, tin cans, copper, and so on—where machines do most of the work (which is the opposite of labor intensive) could be run by the laws of the Medes and the Persians, that is, by rules that are as complete as possible. This, it was thought, aided precision. The machine was precise, so why not the rules? This sounds logical enough.

But what it overlooks is that if any humans are involved at all, the effect on them of machinelike consistency is little short of formidable. This takes the form of labor organization, strikes, slowdowns, even putting sand in expensive machines. Three large corporations, American Telephone and Telegraph, General Electric, and General Motors, for example, were slow to learn the dangers of human neglect, whereas Standard Oil Company of New Jersey (now Exxon) was one of the first to emphasize the greater importance of human motivation over machine regularity.

The universal discovery now is that the more machine dominated the industry is, the more attention, relatively, it must give to human relations if efficiency and morale are to be maintained. This contrasts with the lawyers' disposition in recent years to insist that the more rules there are, the better, because that is the way to assure uniformity even in the smallest details. In both cases the mistake is made of pushing a logical argument too far.

It also is sometimes argued that when a program is new and is struggling to get established, the government should deliberately hold off in its intensive rule making. In other words, more discretion is needed in the early stages than in the later. This argument is partly fallacious. It is right concerning the early stages, but wrong concerning the later ones. The older an organization is, the more it tends to rely on habit and stops thinking. Rules speed up this process. Hence the better policy is this: the older the organization and the better it has been run over the years, the more it should attempt to dispense with needless rules and substitute employee education and a resulting sense of responsibility.[1]

On the observations that have been made, there is an impressive degree of agreement among academics and practitioners. Many of these have written on comparative administration, by which is meant corporate and government administration, although it also may include labor organization, church administration, military administration, and other institutions as is true in this book.

A convenient starting point might be Daniel Wren's book, *The Evolution of Management Thought* (1972). Then, especially if one were a lawyer and wanted a hard-nosed analysis, I would recommend *Management by Results* (1961) by Edward C. Schleh. Then there is a book by some Harvard Business School professors (Learned, Ulrich, and Booz) that I like very much, *Executive Action* (1951), because, on the basis of case studies, it shows the degree to which even business administration is political and why it is that excessive rules sap the life of management. A similar book, for government, because it traces out the strategy of a case study, is my own *The Executive in Action* (1945). Finally, if I wanted to learn why negative factors such as rules are debilitating and what positive psychological incentives work better, I would turn to an early book of David Selznick called *Leadership in Administration* (1957). There are literally scores of books one might read. I mention these because they deal with certain issues I have been raising.

I have said that the administrator is guided by policy. Let me be more explicit about what I mean. In my book mentioned above, we in war shipping had but one main objective: to help win the war by assuring skilled manpower for Allied ships all over the world. Some examples of policies were these: to treat union and nonunion operators the same; to require physical examinations for gunners but to make sure that these examinations were not used to discriminate against unions; to give blacks and whites equal treatment so long as they held the same skill certificates; to concentrate on returning skilled seamen to sea duty instead of training fresh recruits because that was a more efficient use of scarce manpower; to hold a certain number of skilled men on standby pay all over the world because failure to do so might lose a battle; when men were ashore in facilities we owned, to give them responsibility for maintaining order because in the last analysis only they could hope to succeed; after battle fatigue, to get our men out of our psychiatric facilities as soon as the doctors approved, because activity is an offset to depression; and, finally, to hold meetings of operators and unions before promulgating any policy like those mentioned, because if they had it sprung on them, they probably would do everything possible to embarrass us.

These are policies. By no stretch of the imagination are they rules. But because lawyers as a whole are so inexperienced in administration, they make the mistake of lumping everything together under a common rubric and then assume that if rules are ever good, the more of them there are the better things will go. They go well for the Washington lawyer's pocketbook, but for no one else's.

If I may be nautical again, a policy is like a lighthouse on which the seafarer takes his reckonings. It doesn't tell him in detail what he has to do, but it does tell him how much latitude for success or failure he has. That is the way he likes it.

Let me conclude this discussion of the administrator's mystique by making two observations. This is aimed at those who may be skeptical about the primacy of the synthesis factor in executive work. The first is to point out that in some countries where I have done technical assistance work, executive skills are in amazingly short supply among the indigenous population. When one looks into this, one finds three common explanations: the country has been dominated from the outside for centuries, as India was; second, liberty is such a new thing that only a miniscule number of individuals have had the freedom and broad experience from which executive skills emanate; or third, those countries where executive traits are hardest to produce are the ones in which, often for religious reasons, rules dominate peoples' lives and initiative is discouraged. In short, do not expect initiative where there are too many rules. People walk around as if in a stupor.

My second observation again has to do with relevant reading. One of the best (and earliest) explanations of why the ability to synthesize and direct organizations is such a rare skill came from the pen of Chester Barnard, who was trained as a psychologist and was an official of the Bell System for many years, rising to a company presidency. In an essay called "Mind in Everyday Affairs," which is an appendix to his book *The Functions of the Executive* (1938), Barnard finds the synthesizing ability in a combination of rationality/logic and experiential/intuition. With sheer logic, you can go only so far, and if you press too hard beyond this point, you wind up with incomplete and unworkable solutions (that is why, despite all the talk to the contrary, the computer will never replace the human mind).

In the executive, the logic ability is more successful if the person is able to go quickly to the heart of problems instead of meandering through a web of theoretical formalism. Second, says Barnard, the ultimate solution is based upon intuition. This is because intuition is not necessarily "soft." It is based upon a great deal of experience, with intuition as both process and product. Moreover, without this so-called nonrational component, it is doubtful if the executive would be able to respond to projections of future developments, to the values that figure in the public's evaluation of success and legitimacy, and to the psychological factors that to the engineer or the logician are frequently so baffling. In short, the nonrational is par excellence the realm of sensitivity. The logician may approach it, but he never excels in it. The executive is an unusual fellow therefore because he is both logical and intuitive. This combination makes him integrative and capable of leading and inspiring others. This same fusion of opposites makes him realize, as he soon would anyhow from experience, that policies are his friends and a proliferation of detailed rules are his lilliputian enemies.

NOTE

1. These two propositions are explained in greater detail in two of my books, *The Executive in Action* (1945) and *Administrative Vitality: The Conflict with Bureaucracy* (1959) (both published by Harper & Row).

— 4 —

THE ADMINISTRATOR'S VIEW OF THE LAW

To the public administrator, law is something very positive and concrete. It is his authority. The term he customarily uses to describe it is "my mandate." It is "his" law, something he feels a proprietary interest in. It does three things: tells him what the legislature expects him to accomplish, fixes limits to his authority, and sets forth the substantive and procedural rights of the individual and group. Having a positive view of his mandate, the administrator considers himself both an interpreter and a builder. He is a builder because every time he applies old law to new situations he builds the law. Therefore law, like administration, is government in action. It is operational, functional, sociological.

Like the judge, the administrator "finds" the law. Around 1940, when we in the Immigration Service of the Justice Department decided to develop an administrative manual for our field officials as an adjunct to their training, this is the logical way we proceeded: What is our statutory authority? What is the ruling case law as found in court cases that serve as precedents? What are our own sublegislative or policy interpretations of statutory authority by means of which we give effect to steps in the administrative unfolding of the law not specifically provided in the words of the statute? Behind the statutory authority and controlling and limiting it, what is our constitutional authority? What standards of fairness as found in administrative due process of law are we expected to observe? What internal standards of administration are we prepared to follow in order to give fuller effect to the foregoing?

It is like a flow chart in which one thing leads to another and all have a smooth unfolding. Law, to the administrator, is not something outside his work, boring in on him. Rather, it is an integral part of his unfolding plan and strategy of accomplishment.

Looked at this way, namely, as the logical development of a work process, many of the questions that continue to agitate the jurist and political philosopher seem to resolve themselves automatically. The public administrator has taken an oath to observe equally the statutory and the constitutional law, and he is in no doubt that the constitutional law has a higher binding effect. But he regards the statutory law fully as important and deserving of faithful compliance. He knows from his daily experience that both morality and duty are involved in every step of his work. He soon learns that in everything he does, private and public interest must be kept in balance. So sometimes he thinks about the philosophy of the law and the field of jurisprudence, with its age-old problems. We tried to underscore these questions in the training program we ran for immigrant inspectors, naturalization examiners, border patrolmen, and all our personnel. We realized that the more we concentrated on law, the less likely it was that lawyers and judges outside the organization would try to tell us how to run our business.

There are lawyers who have understood this. Ernst Freund, one of the early pioneers in administrative law, hit the nail squarely on the head when he said, "Law is the orderly adjustment of human affairs" (*Encyclopedia of the Social Sciences*, vol. 4, p. 347). Roscoe Pound, although he objected to the view that law is whatever is done by those who wield the power of politically organized society, warned in his *Contemporary Juristic Theory* (1940), " . . . government must be able to do things and administration paralyzed by law is not an enduring political condition" (p. 28). My former boss in Justice, Robert H. Jackson, later a Supreme Court justice, used even stronger language in his book, *The Struggle for Judicial Supremacy* (1941):

> The legal profession does not have the comprehensive wisdom to govern all society. [It tends to become overprofessionalized, for example.] We forget that law is the rule for simple and untaught people to live by. We complicate and over-refine it as a weapon in legal combat until we take it off the ground where people live and into the thin atmosphere of sheer fiction (pp. 291–92).

Then he concludes, "The conventional case or controversy procedure is inadequate to collect, summarize, and interpret the experience and reason of our society" (p. 298).

In other words, both the better administrators and the better lawyers have a common respect for the law and for each other. This is not to say that administrators are unconcerned with the controversies that have been taking place amongst legal philosophers in recent years, because they cannot help but be.

It matters a great deal whether law is considered primarily rules or primarily principles, and these are the two main schools of jurisprudence that have been struggling for supremacy. Second, there are those who contend that legislative-made law has a lower standing than the higher law that comes from natural law, historic landmarks like Magna Carta, the whole body of common law traditions, and people's moral views of private rights and property. Some call this inchoate body of law a myth or fiction; but whether myth or reality it constantly affects the administrator's life.

The administrator's natural inclination is to side with those who think about law as principle and policy, because that is the way his mind works. So when Ronald Dworkin of Harvard says that when you deal with obligation you deal not only or even principally with rules, because more largely you deal with standards, principles, policies, and other sorts of standards,[1] that makes sense to the administrator.

It is the positivist view of law, which started with John Austin's idea of sovereignty, that is the source of most of the administrator's complaints. The logic runs like this: the political state is the fount of all authority and compulsion; the state makes rules affecting all of human behavior; the more human behavior is controlled by rules the more central law will be; there are various kinds of rules, but all set out to limit or eliminate discretion; therefore anyone who cannot cite a rule to justify his acts is outside the law.[2]

To the political theorist, this chain of logic is the perfect example of logic carried to extreme lengths and not balanced by equally valid considerations. The conservatives are particularly bemused. They complain the loudest about how wicked government regulation is, how it invades one area after another, and yet these same people have more to do with burdening business, labor, and all areas of life with rules and regulations than the administrators who are derisively called "the bureaucrats."

It seems much more reasonable to argue, as J. Roland Pennock and John W. Chapman do in their book, *The Limits of Law* (1974), that sometimes public opinion is stronger than law. In such cases attempts at enforcement are eventually given up. The claimed regularity of life conflicts with the variety of life and hence the paradox: to do justice requires that law be limited. For in the last analysis, say Pennock and Chapman, law is limited in two ways, by "is" and "ought" (preface, p. 6).

To the same effect is a cryptic remark of Mr. Justice Cardozo in *The Nature of the Judicial Process* (1922): " . . . when a rule, after it has been duly tested by experience, has been found to be inconsistent with the sense of justice or with the social welfare, there should be less hesitation in frank avowal and full abandonment" (p. 150). Or these admonitions of Roscoe Pound, who in the later stages of his life came to be regarded as something of a conservative in jurisprudence:

> More and more in the ordering of conduct, especially in the conduct of enterprises, the law relies today on standards rather than rules— Application of standards and interpretations are done with reference to received ideals, authoritative pictures of the social order which are as much a part of the law as rules and principles and conceptions (*Contemporary Juristic Theory*, 1940, p. 82).

To this and to the Cardozo admonition, the administrator says, "Hurrah—that's what we think, too!"

On the first of the two great issues about which modern-day jurists such as Lon Fuller, and the Englishman H. L. A. Hart argue so heatedly, namely principles versus rules, the administrator says, "both," but with rules not being pushed to extreme lengths, where they act as a constant burden on initiative and problem solving.

To the same effect are two recent statements of the Chief Justice of the Supreme Court, Warren E. Burger. On May 17, 1977, he observed to the American Law Institute, "Courts are thought to be a stabilizing force in society, but they cannot be static instruments. They are tools, not ends in themselves. Their function is to respond to needs. As needs change, courts must change." And again at the Pound Conference in St. Paul, Minnesota, in April 1976 (70 Federal Rules Decisions 79), the Chief Justice said:

> Ever since Magna Carta, common law lawyers have recognized that the law is a generative mechanism sharing with nature the capacity for growth and adaptation. The changes in seven and a half centuries since then demonstrate that change is a fundamental law of life and even our need for stability and continuity must yield to that immutable law. What is important is that lawyers fulfill their responsibility to preside over orderly evolution. It is now up to us to demonstrate whether we will be able to adapt the basically sound mechanisms of our system of laws to new conditions and abandon those that are obsolete.

The second issue identified above, namely, whether common law is somehow superior to the mandate given the administrator by the legislature, touches the administrator in an even more sensitive spot. This doctrine causes him to consider two things: first, he wonders if the United States is living under representative government or under a government by lawyers; second, his work is made more difficult because he needs a clear mandate, which legislation passed by Congress gives him, and doesn't like to be surprised when so-called higher law, on occasion, upsets this certainty. The doctrine is an old one and has a great deal to do with the attempt to convert the public law of administrative law into private law, and hence it is central to major concerns as one attempts to develop reconciliations.

Strange to say, the doctrine of common law superiority over the statutory law has even more supporters in Great Britain than it does in the United States. This is surprising because since the early seventeenth century, it supposedly has been a settled principle of English constitutional law that parliamentary supremacy is an established fact. But so strong is the fear of instruments of the state being above the law in Britain, and thus depriving citizens of their natural rights, that this doctrine still persists.

For example, Justice Scarman in his Hamlyn Lectures (*English Law—The New Dimension*, 1974) says that English law is lawyer's law. In theory, there are no gaps of omission. *Doctor Bonham's Case* tried to establish the superiority of courts over legislation, but failed (p. 2). Despite this, Scarman contends:

> The modern English judge still sees enacted law as an exception, a graft upon, or a correction of, the customary law in his hands. . . . He interprets laws of Parliament against a backdrop of an all-embracing customary law (p. 3).

He then goes on to state quite frankly that it is because Parliament merely "amends" the customary law that attempts to codify law (as continental countries do and the United States has to a considerable extent) "have always been resisted" (p. 4). Then this: "The artifice of the lawyers makes the rules, and faced with the choice between certainty and flexibility, the judges will choose the former, even if it be shown to operate harshly or even unjustly" (pp. 6,7). This is obviously strong language, especially when Scarman uses the term "unjustly."

Reviewing Scarman's book, Nevil Johnson states quite sensibly that since the common law, which is "arcane and technical," is essentially concerned with private relationships, into which somehow or other its inevitable concern with public matters is "uncomfortably squeezed," what is needed is a new education in public law directed to an understanding of the terms on which individuals and the public authority interact. This takes the form of finding the principles by which to judge this interaction critically, and to an appreciation of the ways in which law both expresses and can change social and economic relationships.[3]

What this public law called administrative law is and should be, will be developed in a later chapter of this book.

The same stubbornness toward legislative law has been found continuously, though somewhat sporadically, since the U.S. Constitution was adopted in 1789. However, except during a few notable periods, mainly the New Deal period, it has not been so much a challenge to legislative authority as something else. First is the "right reason" doctrine enunciated by Chief Justice John Marshall in many of his landmark decisions and as explained in depth by Charles Grove Haines in his book (suggested by Roscoe Pound), *The Revival of Natural Law Concepts* (1930). There is some natural law content in Scarman's and others' thinking, but it is outweighed by parochial pride in the distinctiveness of English institutions. This element of national pride has been clearly brought out in Nevil Johnson's book, *In Search of the Constitution*, published in Britain in 1977. But whether called natural law or something else, there is a large element of this bias in explaining the resistance to legislative supremacy on both sides of the Atlantic. The other factor, of course, is the U.S. doctrine of judicial supremacy, initiated by Chief Justice Marshall in his 1803 decision of *Marbury* v. *Madison*, and enunciated from time to time ever since, especially during the New Deal period. This doctrine is fully explained in Haines's *The American Doctrine of Judicial Review* (2d ed., 1932) and Robert K. Carr's *The Supreme Court and Judicial Review* (1942).

The more recent espousal of common law supremacy, however, is attributable to those who, like Alexander Bickel and F. A. Hayek, are suspicious of "social justice" and hence rely upon the doctrine of innate human rights, much as Hobbes did.

The most extreme presentation of this thesis—although he calls it liberal—is that of Hayek in his two-volume work, *Law, Legislation, and Liberty: A New Statement of the Liberal Principles of Justice and Political Economy* (1973).

Hayek's bête noire is social legislation, or what he calls "welfare" legislation, which has proliferated in recent years in the United States. It is also sometimes called "social justice." Hayek draws a sharp line between legislative law and the kind of law he favors. In volume one he explains his opposition to statutory law and in so doing also shows the connection between this and his view of administrative law, which, as noted earlier, is the basic reason that Bernard Schwartz takes a narrow view of what is involved in administrative law.

Hayek's objection is to goal-directed administration, which, as has been seen, is the essence of the administrator's strategy and what allows him to unify his work and make it effective. Hayek is opposed to goals because they sound too authoritarian. Hayek is opposed to "the socialization of the law." He puts the blame for socialization on the legislature and those who call themselves public administrators. "When we speak of administrative measures," says Hayek, "we generally mean the direction of particular resources towards the rendering of certain services to determinable groups of people" (p. 139). He distinguishes this with the economist's alternative approach, which is toward "policy." However, as has been pointed out previously, this is also the administrator's point of view, and hence Hayek assumes things that are either not true of the administrator or that ought instead to be charged to the legal profession.

His general position is that there are two kinds of law, public and private. The private is the "real" law. Since there can be only one body of "real" law, it follows that laws of government are like "by-laws." Similarly with the Constitution (and by necessary inference, constitutional law)—the Constitution is simply "super-structure." He then argues that administrative law is "the main part" of public law. But what is it? Here Hayek takes even a narrower view than those law school professors such as Schwartz. He defines administrative law as "the rules of *organization* that affect public accountability." It also deals with sublegislation. It has become important because of social legislation. Therefore, says Hayek, "It is the part of the law lawyers like least." Why? In his words, "It infringes on the common law and tends to overshadow it" (I, pp. 131–39, at 139).

Hayek's reasoning is very confusing because it is distorted by his initial antagonism toward social legislation in all its forms. When he deals with the administrative implications of his principles, for example, he suddenly begins to think like an economist and not one who is prejudiced against government and all its works. This is particularly evident when he deals with the controversial subject of rule versus principle, where his views would be widely applauded by the public administrator. For example:

> Principles do not necessarily take the form of articulated rules (I, p. 60).
> A rule is simply "a propensity or disposition to act or not act in a

certain manner, which will manifest itself in what we call a practice or custom" (I, p. 75).

An "order" describes a state of affairs in which a multiplicity of elements of various kinds are so related to each other that we may learn from our acquaintance with some spatial or temporal part of the whole to form certain correct expectations concerning the rest, or at least expectations that have a good chance of proving correct" (I, p. 36).

In any group of more than the smallest size, collaboration will always rest both on spontaneous order as well as on deliberate organization (I, p. 46).

It is in a condition of liberty, where all are allowed to use their knowledge for their purposes, restrained only by rules of just conduct of universal application, that the group is most likely to produce the best conditions for achieving their aims" (I, p. 55).

If you were to take a poll of all members of the National Academy of Public Administration, most likely there would be very little dissent from these principles!

Like so many administrative lawyers, Hayek would spare himself a great deal of difficulty if he would merely state that he is opposed to social legislation and attempts to secure social justice, and let it go at that. Those in the public administration profession could even subscribe to one of his main dicta in volume II, "Abstract rules operate as ultimate values because they serve unknown particular ends" (II, p. 48).

A good example of this would be the attempt to undermine social legislation by lawyers' associations by means of making public administration cumbersome and ineffective, through excessive rules and formal procedures, after they have lost the initial round in the legislature where the legislation was passed.

The case of Alexander Bickel in *The Morality of Consent* (1975) is also germane and interesting, though not so extreme. After disposing of the notion that values are derived from religion or natural law, Bickel enunciates the doctrine of legal omniscience:

The irreducible value, though not the exclusive one, is law. Law is more than just another opinion; not because it embodies all right values, or because the values it does embody tend from time to time to reflect those of a majority or plurality, but because it is the value of values. Law is the principal institution through which society can assert its values (p. 5).

This is a good example of myth building, but an equally poor exposition of the sociology of law.

Bickel's contribution to administrative thinking is found in the following points. There are no principles because they tend toward authoritarianism. Therefore a government of rules is wrong. Since rules are wrong, then the only thing that is right is a process that allows for continuity, pragmatic decision, adjustment, and change. He reiterates that he does not believe in or trust religion. He does trust interest, self-interest, and, like laissez-faire philosophers of old (but not Adam Smith), believes that this is the surest guarantee of freedom.

Bickel proves himself a thorough liberal. But I should hate to try to administer programs if I believed in all of his injunctions. He comes close to deserving the epithet that women employ against men, chauvinist. He is one who thinks that all virtue is found in law but is never sure what it is.

What has been argued in this chapter is that the administrator has a broad, receptive attitude toward law and its hierarchy, but has little use for fictions or myths that can be seized upon by selfish interests to undermine his effectiveness. Two of these areas of controversy were examined: the idea that law is nothing but rules, and the opposing view that it is principle and policy. There is some value in both points of view. Then considered was the question of the nature of law, whether it is mainly statutory and case law, based upon the Constitution, as the administrator assumes, or whether it is an inchoate body of belief and custom confined almost entirely to private or common law. It was recognized that there are many sources of law and hence many varieties of specialization, but the idea that law is wholly private was found to be unacceptable. Nor was it accepted that there are two kinds of law and that public law deals entirely with organization and is hence of a lower order of nature, dealing almost entirely with administration. Finally, as a rule it is not the law that the administrator is most suspicious of; it is the lawyer and how he often manipulates the law to his own selfish ends that the administrator mistrusts.

NOTES

1. Ronald Dworkin, "Is Law a System of Rules?" *Essays in Legal Philosophy*, ed. Robert S. Summers (Berkeley: University of California Press, 1968), p. 34.

2. H. L. A. Hart, *The Concept of Law* (Oxford: Oxford University Press, 1961).

3. Nevil Johnson, "Editorial: Law and the Constitution: A Judge's Warning," *Journal of Public Administration* (London) 51 (Autumn 1975): 221–29, at p. 226.

— 5 —

THE LAWYER'S VIEW OF THE LAWYER

Ours is a lawyer-dominated society. Bernard Schwartz doubtless was not overstating the case when he made that claim in his *Administrative Law* (1976).

Among the reasons for the lawyer's influence the following are common knowledge. First, their number, which is far more than in other countries. Second, their strategic role and dominance or near dominance in all three branches of government. Third, their dispersion throughout the economy, because more law school graduates go into industry, government, and all fields of economic life outside of legal practice than are engaged in the actual arguing and deciding of cases and controversies. Fourth, their reputation, mostly deserved, for being wielders and manipulators of power, especially in the corporate field, where the largest number of them earn large salaries or wind up running corporate empires. Fifth, their ability to play both ends against the middle—they, more than any other group, make the statutory law and impose the interferences on various areas of the economy, requiring an equally large number of their brethren to advise these same regulated interests on how to circumvent governmental interference.

If there is not enough work for a growing number of lawyers, they have enough knowhow and political savvy to see that government provides the extra work. Finally, perhaps the most important factor of all is a psychological one. Instead of being trained as formerly in an apprenticeship system that kept them fairly modest, they are now trained in law schools, where their egos and self-confidence are enhanced. The unwritten law of the legal profession is that the lawyer has the potential to deal with any technology, from physics to medicine and from psychiatry to insurance, because he is resourceful and adapts quickly. He may not know, but he is expected to act as though he did. He knows he is not omniscient, but protocol requires that he act as if he thought he were. He likes a cockfight. But like the minister or the physician, he also soothes people's fears in times of trouble.

In a profession so neatly adjusted to natural selection, it is perhaps not surprising that new law schools are created every year or that those who start them exude confidence that there is no foreseeable limit to how many lawyers the country needs.

But there is beginning to be a reaction against the legal profession's overweening influence, and it is by no means confined to the beleaguered public administrator. For example, in a special issue of *Iron Age* (April 1978) entitled, "Life in the State Regulatory Jungle and How it Has Business in a Bind," the main complaint is rules—and the lawyers who make them:

> Does government really want everyone in industry to be a lawyer? ... If any single attorney tried to read any state's complete repertoire [of rules] he'd spend his whole life in the library.... Federal rules. State Rules. County rules. Local rules. Rules revised. Rules written, rewritten, interpreted and re-interpreted.

"The list of rules and regulations is not endless," concludes this article. "A few million good lawyers could surely list them all, every word." Then the author says that in rule making, the states are the clear winners compared to Washington, D.C. After all, there are fifty state legislatures but only one Congress. The article concludes by saying, "The most insidious aspect of the whole regulatory mess is that we're becoming frighteningly cynical about law in general."

Call some of this exaggeration if you will. But ask any production executive in industry and you will find a substantial degree of agreement. It is not only the government administrator's ox that is being gored!

It was not always thus. In fact, the problem has become acute only during the past generation, and then as a reaction to the New Deal. Among other countermeasures, this reaction took the form of the Administrative Procedure Act of 1946, epitomizing the bar associations' triumph at both the federal and the state levels. There has been a great deal of regulatory legislation of the Ralph Nader-type also, but the two are bound up together. Nader's "boys" infiltrate the government just as other lawyers do.

The historical perspective that is needed to provide guidance for future professional policy in the legal field runs somewhat as follows. There have been five main periods in the evolution of the legal profession in the United States. From 1789 until after the Civil War, the number of lawyers was small, they were mostly apprentice trained in law offices, and the legal profession was frequently compared to the ministry. They were the educated class and much respected. They had a strong sense of duty and of public interest.

The second period, beginning about 1870 and extending to the New Deal, saw the emergence of large corporations and the passage of the Interstate Commerce Commission Act of 1887 and the Sherman Antitrust Act of 1890. It was around this time that lawyers began to gravitate to "the interests" and to be less closely identified with public custodianship than formerly.

During the third period, extending from the New Deal to the end of World War II, lawyers gained a reputation for boring from within the government as legislators, judges, and watchdogs of administration.

The fourth period, commencing soon after the end of World War II, saw two quite dissimilar developments. Lawyers played a large part in the growth of conglomerates and transnational corporations, and second, they became much involved with civil rights, especially during the Warren Court period.

Beginning some time in the 1960s, a new or fifth phase seems to be emerging, with young lawyers much interested in public interest law. Were there not so many lawyers who need to be employed, somehow this might possibly augur a return to phase one, when again the legal profession's interest centered on public responsibility.

The trends in the legal profession that Adolf Berle of Columbia University Law School called attention to in 1933 are even more pronounced today. Public regard for the legal profession is lower now than when Berle wrote. In his article on "Legal Profession and Legal Education" (*Encyclopedia of the Social Sciences*, vol. 5), Berle draws a picture of a large law firm—even the ones with the most prestige—as being the "paid hirelings" of the largest corporations. As a result, Berle argued that the tradition of public service and the ethical standards of the profession have declined appreciably. He refers to lawyers as "jobbers and contractors," with virtually no independence, instead of their being, as formerly, "a moral force."

I lived through this period, too, and knew many lawyers. I think that possibly Berle overgeneralized and drew too pessimistic a picture. However, it is easy to overgeneralize and I am often guilty of it, so perhaps I should not criticize.

In the last few years (even months) a number of things have been done to correct this unfavorable reputation: the leaders of the bar, led by Chief Justice Burger, have spoken out openly and strongly; in February 1978 the American Bar Association approved a set of standards to punish and oust unfit judges (New York *Times*, February 15, 1978); and the required teaching of required courses on legal ethics was recommended by the American Association of Law Schools.

Burger has led the fight to limit the number of lawyers, to raise the standard of ethics for the profession, in particular for trial lawyers, and generally to restore the profession to its former respected role. The key to all these reforms, he believes, is reducing the excessive number of lawyers. "Burger Warns about a Society Overrun by Lawyers," says an article appearing in the New York *Times* of May 28, 1977. During the same month the chief judge of the New York State Court of Appeals, as reported in the same article, stated that, "if lawyers just grab, grab, grab, they may be killing the goose that lays the golden egg." I do not know what Justice Breitel meant by this, but if he meant undermining the free enterprise system and public confidence in representative government, I must reluctantly agree with him.

According to Laurin A. Wollan, Jr., in 1978 there were 445,000 lawyers in the United States, and the law schools were producing new ones so fast that by 1985 the number is expected to be 600,000. In the federal government alone, there are upward of 50,000 lawyers, an increase from around 27,000 in 1951.[1] It was the Administrative Procedure Act of 1946 that did much to make Washington the lawyer's paradise. In terms of sources of recruitment for the public service, lawyers lead professionally trained economists and public administrators by a large margin. Hence, statistically, the best way to become a government executive is to be a lawyer, although law school may provide the worst preparation.

The bare statistics, though impressive, do not begin to convey the full impression. But Burger has seen to that. There is by far a higher percentage of lawyers to the total population in the United States than in any other country. In 1978 it was reported that 110,000 new lawyers had been turned out of the country's 105 law schools in seven years, a far greater rate of growth than for the population as a whole. The number of practicing lawyers per 100,000 population reveals that the United States has 14 times as many as Japan, for example, where some effective means have been found to solve controversies and do justice without going to court so frequently. In 1975 alone there were 33,000 graduates from law schools in the United States. In England the number of lawyers is kept very small because they are divided into two groups, barristers and solicitors; there is a centralized and comprehensive training facility for all trial lawyers, and admission of lawyers to practice law in courts of general jurisdiction is coordinated in a central governing body.[2] As a result, in 1975 England had only 33,000 solicitors and barristers, whereas the United States had over ten times that many.

The historical perspective as revealed in an October 1976 *Harper's* article, "A Plague of Lawyers," helps to complete the picture. According to Jerald S. Auerbach,

> At the beginning of the century there was approximately one lawyer for every 1,100 Americans (1:1100). Twenty-five years ago it was 1:700. In 1976 it was 1:530.

Since 1970, says Auerbach, the population grew by 6 percent, the legal profession by 14 percent. In 1950 there were 53,000 law students, in 1973, 97,000.

Justice Burger is always at great pains to point out that "lawyers and judges have made and are making great contributions to achieving a fair and humane society," but he also warns that if some areas do not devise substitutes for the formal, lengthy, and expensive courtroom process, and do it rather quickly, the United States may well be on its way to a society overrun with "hordes of locusts" competing with each other, and "brigades of judges" in numbers never before contemplated.

Finally, not only do lawyers increasingly outnumber executives in the federal government, but they also continue to be the largest single professional group in Congress and in state legislatures. In 1978, out of the 7,564 men and women who comprised the legislatures of the 50 states, 22 percent were lawyers, with Virginia leading the list at 57 percent. Finally, two-thirds of the presidents of the United States have been lawyers, and even in President Carter's cabinet as of 1978, nearly half were lawyers. Considering that lawyers dominate all three branches, it is almost literally true that to improve the government the legal profession must be reformed.

The best general treatise on this subject is in Milton Mayer's book, *The Lawyers* (1967), and the best analysis of how large law firms influence both legislation and administration in Washington is Mark J. Green's book, *The Other Government: Unseen Power in Washington* (1975).

The article in the *Public Administration Review*, which has been quoted, was written by a lawyer who concludes on a rather disturbing note. After pointing out that lawyers have been "a bastion of counter-vailing independence and authority in the mosaic of pluralistic powers that is the foundation of free government" (p. 111), he states that if the standards of professionalization continue to decline and lawyers become increasingly indistinguishable from "the milieu of bureaucracy"—the kind that lives exclusively on rules—the legal profession might in time become merely "an instrument of the State." If this should be allowed to occur, it might cause "grievous cost" to itself and to its members in terms of freedom—but not just theirs: the community's and its citizens' as well (p. 111).

What is the role of the Washington lawyer or the law firms that specialize at state capitols or in large cities? Louis M. Kohlmeier, Jr., in his book *The Regulators* (1969), says they are specialists and that they are narrowly trained: "Most Washington lawyers are paid to be specialists, not generalists." (Most government executives, as was seen earlier, are generalists because the nature of their work requires it.) The specialization of the Washington lawyer, says Kohlmeier, "inhibits informed comprehension of the total fabric, which is woven of economic and political as well as legal strands" (p. x).

Green, in *The Other Government*, points out that in the District of Columbia there is one lawyer for every 600 persons in the population. "They have burrowed themselves into the federal establishment" (p. 4). Capital attorneys more frequently draft bills than wills. Most of them concentrate on the administrative agencies that "have come to equal in influence the three formal branches of government—Congress, courts, White House" (p. 5). He quotes with approval Ambrose Bierce's dictum to the effect that "A lawyer is a person skilled in circumvention of the law." There are 35 large law firms of more than 20 attorneys each and they practice "power law" (p. 3). He also subscribes to Ferdinand Lundberg's statement that "most of the deals and misdeeds of the robber-barons were in actuality the mere projections of lawyers' schemes. . . . They are the brains of American capitalism" (p. 4).

These law firms, says Green, "dispense great wealth via licenses, subsidies, contracts, approved rate schedules, or can limit great wealth by tax, antitrust, and regulatory standards." The "Big Six" of the Washington law firms "have direct 'authority' over some $120 billion of commerce" (p. 5). Their gross legal product amounts to $90 billion. Green quotes J. P. Morgan as saying that Elihu Root was "the only lawyer who tells me what I want to do" (pp. 9–10). A partner of Burling and Covington is reported as saying, "I'm for bureaucracy.

How could I do otherwise?" (p. 22). The Washington law firm, says the same partner, "is a culture as well as a law firm" (p. 31). On the controversial question of lawyers going directly from the law firm to the government where they can make their influence felt, he says of a former official of the Food and Drug Administration, "his transfer is comparable to going from poacher to gamekeeper" (p. 30). The strategy of the big law firm, Green notes, is "to wear the government out" (p. 69). Many lawyers sit on the boards of directors of their clients in order to gain a more intimate knowledge of what they are expected to do in government proceedings (p. 59).

He stops short of calling all this a conspiracy. He does believe that it weakens legal ethics and that it is a main cause of the public's lowered regard for the legal profession. A Harris poll made in 1973, for instance, found that of those institutions in which U.S. citizens had confidence, law firms won only 24 percent approval, ranking behind doctors, garbage collectors, organized religion, Congress, local government, and the police (Green, p. 7).

Was the author of the book on Washington lawyers himself a lawyer? Yes. One who favors the pro bono publico law firm, however.

This story of the Washington lawyer obviously uncovers a new dimension in the analysis found in the preceding chapter, where law was considered as a concept or an ideal. The new dimension deals with power and influence. The successful Washington lawyer is a power broker, an entrepreneur, closely resembling the top executives who head industries and labor unions. They make rules for others, but do everything possible to avoid rules for themselves.

Law as power is a universal factor. The late Harold J. Laski, of the London School of Economics and Political Science, once said that the British Labour Party, which became political around the turn of the century, would never gain power until its members produced enough lawyer sons who would learn to manipulate power the way the landed gentry and the industrialists had done for generations past. Marxist theorists are accused of using the law to gain class ends. In recent years, however, the Soviet Union has determinedly insisted that its law and system of justice serve universal principles of fairness and objectivity. They seek the approval of public opinion in other countries. So, similarly, do our most respected leaders of the bar such as Chief Justice Warren Burger, and earlier, men like Brandeis, Cardozo, Hand, Pound, and others.

The United States is peculiarly exposed to greater temptations to use the law—especially administrative law—for economic and class purposes than are most other countries. This is not merely because business and moneymaking are so much stressed—which would

Bernard Schwartz says in his *Administrative Law* (1976), "The Welfare State has converted an ever-growing portion of the community into government clients; Americans are coming increasingly to live on public largess" (p. 6). So another step is taken. Welfare involves private rights and governmental interference, too. (Schwartz's capitalization of Welfare State indicates that.) So, by extension, the whole of the administrative process ought to be judicialized; this is pretty much what has happened since 1946.

The rationale is that private rights are being protected, that is, the rights of the individual under the Constitution. This is unquestionably the motivation of the rank and file of most bar associations. But in many of these bar associations there is also a dominant interest in the corporation as a person under the Fifth and Fourteenth Amendments. With this motivation, and the highest financial stakes in the whole of legal practice at the specialized law firm's command, the public administrator's claims to understanding and equal treatment may, and often do, get short shrift.

It is a power game, and in such games ethics are endangered to a greater degree than in any other category of law. The better judges and practicing attorneys know this to be true. The question for some time has been whether the bar associations can put their own houses in order. It is in an attempt to bring this about that leaders of the bar, led by the chief justice, have been speaking out in no uncertain way.

If the United States should eventually find a different formula for dealing with major regulation, it would be infinitely easier to effect the reconciliation between administrative law and public administration that is being sought. When there is a single industry, the Bell System, with assets of 80 billion dollars and half as many employees as the whole of the federal government, one can easily appreciate how great the political pressures are on (say) the Federal Communications Commission, and indirectly, of course, on the White House and the members of Congress.

In effect, major regulation, which is the present focus of administrative law courses and has been so pretty much since the time that Frankfurter and Davison wrote their casebook in 1937, is more a political than a legal problem. However, it is being treated more like a legal problem than an administrative one. However, it should be treated as a problem of administrative effectiveness if regulation as a formula is going to succeed. An example of this is found in a study called *A New Regulatory Framework* that some young lawyers and I did during the Nixon administration and that was brought out in 1971.

But effective public opinion, which in this case means basically the regulated industries, does not want a new formula, because it would mean either deregulation, which is now being tried in the case of the airlines, or a new form of ownership, either outright public or mixed enterprise. In any of these cases the presently regulated industries in all probability would be run by autonomous corporations. There would not be divided authority as at present. Because there would be unified management, the reasonable expectation is that many of the problems of regulation that citizens and the private sector complain most loudly about, and that the specialized regulatory bar has a great deal to do with bringing into existence, would be obviated completely. Then the focus of administrative law could turn to the whole of the government, as it did originally under the impetus that Frank J. Goodnow gave it. This would greatly assist the improvement of public administration, whereas today administrative law is an antagonist and a dead weight.

The likelihood of the change occurring ultimately will turn on the United States' worldwide fortunes. If major indicators such as the trade balance, the value of the dollar, and the rate of inflation should continue unfavorably, or even worsen, then there might be a tendency to tackle the fundamental causes of poor governmental operations. In such a searching scrutiny, the improvement of administrative performance unquestionably would appear near the top of the list of priorities. When this time comes, the adverse effect of major regulation and the legal profession's complicity in it doubtless would be exposed to a good deal of scrutiny and possible emendation.

Law is a multifaceted thing because it serves several functions. As principles and a reflection of values, it has a certain permanent, stabilizing quality. It is like the role of the ideal in the life of the individual. At the same time, law is one of the main agents of change in any society. As has been seen, it deals with raw power and with certain forms of sophisticated influence, such as Washington lawyers exert. Since law has at least these two contrasting roles, and if lawyers are not to suffer the fate that Shakespeare wished for them, namely, their elimination, it seems fairly clear that as temptation to manipulate and use questionable methods increases with size and prospective rewards, some effective method needs to be found by the legal profession to bolster up the ethics and uprightness of lawyers and judges. It is only because they are considered incorruptible that people respect them in the first place, and tend to put them, especially the courts, on a pedestal. If the legal profession disappoints the public's expectations, then, as often happens, the public's fury will be even greater than if the profession had less prestige at the outset.

It is a tough job to raise standards, and it will take much leadership and outspokenness of the kind that Chief Justice Burger has provided. The immediate interest here, however, is to see a better understanding of lawyers by administrators and a more realistic understanding of the art of administration by lawyers, both united by a common loyalty to the country and its institutions.

NOTES

1. Laurin A. Wollan, Jr., "Lawyers in Government," *Public Administration Review* 38 (March-April 1978): 106.
2. *Annual Report on the State of the Judiciary*, by Chief Justice Warren E. Burger, American Bar Association, p. 5.

— *6* —

PINPOINTING THE CONFLICT
AREAS IN ADMINISTRATION

Because of the differences in mental set that are analyzed in previous chapters, the threat to administrative performance increases proportionally to the dominance of the lawyer's role. When the lawyer, be he solicitor of the department or staff attorney, confines himself to giving legal advice and handling court cases that arise in the course of administrative performance, the collaboration works very well, and the administrator has no complaint. When, however, a person with the lawyer's set of mind is put in a superior (line) position over the administrator, where he tries to deal with policy and objectives and attempts to reduce the administrative process (as he sees it) to rules and procedures, as he has been taught to do, the unity and the motivation to achieve social goals fall off measurably.

I had an unexcelled opportunity to experience this personally between 1938 and 1940. Under a mandate from President Franklin Roosevelt, I was charged with "reforming" and directing the Immigration and Naturalization Service as assistant secretary of Labor, followed by two years in a comparable policy and directing role in the Department of Justice, between 1940 and 1942, after the Service had been transferred from Labor to Justice as part of a reorganization plan of the Bureau of the Budget. Lawyers, and especially the inexperienced ones, were forever trying to tell me what not to do. But my mandate from the president was positive. I had no choice but to fight their interference and attempted domination, which, with the backing of the president and two sympathetic attorneys-general, Robert Jackson and Francis Biddle, I was able to do.

Perhaps the best example of this occurred shortly after the transfer. A law school professor came to me and said, "Justice being the lawyer's department, I think I should be the head of the Immigration Service. You are a public lawyer, true, but have not been admitted to the bar. I would like to concentrate exclusively on *procedure* and I would allow you to deal with *substance* and be in effect the executive officer. But I would be the boss."

I replied that if this were to take place I would have to resign. When I spoke to the attorney-general about the matter, and he consulted the president, my mandate was reinforced.

I mention this partly because this was the year (1940) when the Report of the Attorney-General's Committee on Administrative Procedure appeared and the movement began to strip administration of its policy flexibility and adjudicative powers and vest these in lawyers. What was proposed for Immigration is what, in effect, has been taking place in the government as a whole since that time. The consequence, as I have been arguing, was to make administrative performance considerably less effective during the past 30 years than it was during the 12 years of the New Deal and World War II.

I shall not try to deal with the whole of the philosophy of administration or all of its components as set forth by writers previously mentioned, such as Drucker in *Management: Tasks, Responsibilities, Practices* (1973) or his earlier book, *The Practice of Management* (1956), or my own book, *The Executive in Action* (1945). Instead, I shall be content to probe into a few main areas, such as objectives, organization, planning, control, decision making, sublegislation, procedure, and personnel. This should be sufficient to make my point. I realize that I am leaving out some traditional subjects that are also part of the amalgam, such as budgeting, evaluation of results, and public relations.

ESTABLISHING OBJECTIVES

One of the secrets of dynamic administration involves the setting of objectives as concretely as possible, while at the same time retaining enough flexibility to make adjustments in midstream when unforeseen obstacles or opportunities arise. This is a prime example of the balancing of seemingly opposed factors to achieve the best of both worlds.

The difference between the way the practical administrator and the conventional (especially academic) lawyer think about this subject is illustrated by the Immigration episode to which I have just made reference. President Roosevelt's objectives were these: to make the Service efficient and effective as assurance that Congress' restrictive legislation would be carried out; second, to launch a positive program of education for naturalization and citizenship generally because the war in Europe had started and the loyalty of aliens would have to be secured either by fear or by stressing U.S. values and the dignity of the individual; third, the Service was one of the oldest and most bureaucratic in Washington and Roosevelt wanted it revitalized. In other words, the president was concerned with people, the time factor, and the institution. And the lawyer who wanted my job? He said quite frankly that his sole objective was to experiment with the Supreme Court holding in the *Morgan* case, which was used as an excuse for attempting to judicialize the whole field of public administration. We improved the fairness of our hearings and appeals, too, but it was in the context of a larger range of objectives.

There is considerable evidence that lawyers, as a professional group, find it difficult to think holistically. They are good analysts but their training tends to de-emphasize synthesis, which is the administrator's forte.

One government lawyer recently has expressed this idea as follows: Lawyers, he says, find it difficult to think effectively in "the ecological mode of Policy-making" that is in favor today. They find it quite uncongenial to "array a multiplicity of measures interconnectedly against interrelated aspects of complex difficulties" (Laurin A. Wollan, Jr., "Lawyers in Government," p. 107). To check this belief he not only studied the literature but also consulted a number of professions that had observed lawyers at work in government. An industrial engineer testified that lawyers characteristically think of one item at a time—linearly—instead of in relation to a matrix. Another quoted Thomas Reed Powell, one of Harvard Law School's greats: "If you think you can think about a thing inextricably attached to something else without thinking of the thing which it is attached to, then you have a legal mind." Another witness thought he found the explanation in the fact that lawyers generally argue deductively and from precedent, whereas the practical businessman tends to be empirical and hence becomes a better manager.

The administrator realizes that everything he does in program management relates back to his initial skill in setting targets for a determinate period. His objectives are his product and profit, and everything else is part of his delivery system, as the Pentagon calls it. Hence the practical administrator does not hesitate to change organization, personnel, field organization, product, or anything else if it contributes to the specificness and appeal of his objectives. Since the most important factor in administration is the human factor, which can innovate and look forward and backward in doing so, anything that provides motivation and incentive is of top order. Nothing provides incentive more naturally or compellingly than employees' dedication to objectives, especially if they have had a part in determining them.

Repeating some of the points that have been made and adding others, the profiles of the two professions look something like this:

The Determining of Objectives

Factor	Administrator	Lawyer
Targets	Establishes specific ones; is work oriented.	Seeks consistency; is precedent oriented.
Time	Time conscious; goals set for a determinate period.	Doctrinally oriented; the consistency he seeks is timeless.
Sales	Consumer oriented, whomsoever he may be.	Client specific; the one who pays the fee.
Policy	Politically oriented, toward the entire policy process.	Craft conscious, toward his standing in a profession.
Method	Strategy attuned.	Rigorously dependent upon rule and procedure.
Unity	Holistically inclined, seeking coordination.	Segmentally inclined.
Flexibility	Adaptable, realizing that the unforeseen is inevitable.	Rigidly affixed, seeking certainty and rule.
People	Incentive is his chief ally.	Rules and impersonality.
Discretion	Nothing can be fully determined in advance.	Discretion is a threat to the majesty of the law.

Enterprise	Innovation is the secret of success.	Bureaucratically oriented; if the rules are clear, everything else is the work of clerks.
Substance	Content of public policy, as in engineering, public works, farming, and so on.	Procedure, law is a process and the substance is someone else's concern.

Again, the above relates to types, not exceptions, because individual lawyers often have become excellent executives when they master the technique of shifting gears and stop thinking like lawyers. Something analogous occurs when administrators are converted from administrators and start thinking like legislators.

ORGANIZATION THEORY

Organization is another area of conflict, as shown in the following comparison:

Factor	Administrator	Lawyer
Flow	Distrusts paper organization, work flows and all steps are related.	Stresses control; everything stems from higher authority, by deduction.
Delegation	Only by delegation can energy and initiative be attained throughout.	Centralizes authority, as in a supreme court.
Decentralization	Unifies authority at the action point.	Monopolizes authority at its fount.
Teamwork	Coordination is the secret of success.	Every role is segmentally distinct.
Responsiveness	Outgoing response to sales, customers, human relations.	A government of laws and not of men.

Operations	Centers his strategy around program executives, the line people who are the producers.	Favors the staff person because he is a professional counsellor like himself.
Order	Organization is a means to an end, requiring flexibility.	Organization is an end; hierarchy, like law, is a search for consistency.
Sublegislation	Recognizes that spelling out the statute is essential at every stage.	Claims that the lawyer mentality should dominate this area.
Decision making	An integral part of work flow and found at every level.	If important enough, should be entrusted only to lawyers and administrative law judges.
Personnel	Line officials should control personnel matters as part of a rounded jurisdiction.	Personnel management should be turned over to experts, who are specialists like himself.
Leadership	The unity of elements required for production should be found at all levels of organization.	If roles and jurisdictions are rigorously delineated, leadership and coordination will occur automatically.
Coordination	This is a constant at every level and on a continuous basis.	Favors a super-agency with the power to command from the top.
Evaluation	The acid test is the degree to which policy and management release energy throughout the organization and achieve efficiency, teamwork, and production.	Favors subordination and tight control to such an extent that accountability becomes the sole object of success.

Commenting on this area of organization theory, a government biologist noted that since lawyers typically argue in a hierarchical manner from constitution, statutes, and cases, and become tradition bound, their object appears to be "to find one's way through a maze without causing it to show a tilt." Still others stated that lawyers are so detail minded and so concerned with the abstract meaning of words that it is frequently difficult to get them to take a stand, whereas the executive's mentality is just the opposite of this (Wollan, p. 108).

THE PLANNING FUNCTION

Now that objectives and organization have been dealt with, perhaps the remaining analyses can be compressed into a briefer compass.

Factor	Administrator	Lawyer
Integration	Plans are made to be used and are of several kinds: product, work, long range, intermediate, shorter term.	Plans are like codes of law: timeless and designed to assure top control.
Instrumental	Relevant planning is designed to keep planning to a minimum: only those things that need to be planned are planned.	Planning is perfection. If a little is good, more is better.
Two-way	Strategic planning starts at the bottom, where production takes place, proceeds to the top, and then comes down again. It is a collaborative effort in which everyone has his input.	Lawyer planning is formalistic; it is top management he serves and it is they who pay his fees.
Voluntarism	Teamwork requires participation, alternative strategies, rapid changes in direction. Resourcefulness is the key.	Control is the goal; it should be undivided and complete, appealing to the Big Man myth.

| Position | Planning should always be as close to the scene of operations as possible. | Planning should be at the apex of the pyramid. |

Much of the reorganization efforts of recent years, at both the state and federal levels, reflects the mental set of the lawyer and not the practical business executive. It is a myth that one man, the president of the United States, can run a huge, sprawling bureaucracy. A business executive who argued this way would soon be laughed out of court.

MANAGERIAL CONTROL

Another important conflict area is control:

Factor	Administrator	Lawyer
Information	Constant, reliable information is needed to determine if the work program is on schedule, whether cost and profit calculations are reliable, and where additional energy and supervision are needed.	Subordination is the key; control is enforced by rules and subrules that if rigidly carried out will assure the dominance of the individual with ultimate responsibility.
Direct contact	Face-to-face contacts are the best assurance that work is being accomplished according to policy agreements.	Adherence to predetermined plans and rules is the objective. The lawyer analogizes to a higher court.
Responsibility	Individual responsibility is basic to motivation and performance. The only way to encourage junior executives is to "give them their heads." If they are challenged they must learn to take risks.	The lawyer believes in safe people, the ones who will follow rules and accept precedents without question. They become the "time-servers" and the bureaucrats the public objects to so much.

| Paperwork | The administrator attempts to reduce paperwork to a minimum as he trusts those beneath him and delegates authority. | Being an expert in procedure, the lawyer's instinctive reliance on rules ends up in red tape. Every time a small problem arises, his gut reaction is to promulgate a new rule. |

There may be only one problem in a hundred where a rule is necessary, but the lawyer's instinct is to broaden it to include everyone. The lawyer knowingly or unwittingly expects practical executives to spend most of their time studying rules and subrules instead of concentrating all their energies on production, and taking care of the exceptions by merely using intelligence, persuasion, the fear of firing, discipline, or a broad Irish grin.

The executive believes that everything in administration is capable of measurement, either quantitatively or qualitatively. He studies results through time and by comparison with analogous situations, with an eye on trends. The lawyer, in comparison, is concerned almost exclusively with adherence to rigid rules and standards, even though they neglect the qualitative factor. Accordingly, as organizations become faceless, the agency becomes less than human.

DECISION MAKING

Because decision making is part of the administrator's overall philosophy of administration, according to which he tries to integrate and unify his work, this subject must be dealt with fully enough at this point to show the connection with other major elements of administration. Decision making and sublegislation are major conflict areas in the approaches of practical administrators and administrative lawyers.

Factor	Administrator	Lawyer
Universality	Decision is a universal need of administration and arises daily and at all levels. These decisions are of varying degrees of	Decisions are detached, atomistic, because the lawyer analogizes to courts of law. In trying to make certain

importance, but all are related and hence if detached destroy the administrator's overall strategy.

decisions concerning property and rights his monopoly, the lawyer winds up attempting to judicialize the entire field of program management. He fractures the needed unity of management.

Values

Because of his mental set, the administrator characteristically deals with a larger range of values than the lawyer. Among these is a respect for human values. The administrator's stock-in-trade is human relations and policy.

The focus is almost entirely on personal rights, with the consequent neglect of social rights. Because of the fact that the Bill of Rights applies to "legal" persons as well as "natural" ones, the concern for human rights is easily translated into political interpretations that favor property, profits, and corporate power and privilege.

Relatedness

Any decision is an integral part of the complex of factors involved in providing dynamic administration. His expertise is largely substantive. In his eyes any overruling of his expertness in this area is as wrong in principle as the overruling of a surgeon's or engineer's professional expertness.

Analogizing to the corpus of law and the function of a court, the lawyer seeks to monopolize decision, assuming that he, alone, is qualified. Because of his attitude of omniscience, he constantly invades the professional competence of other professional experts. He overlooks the substantive expertness of the administrator, and although professing to be interested only in procedure does not neglect the substantive interests of his clients.

| Hearing | Giving a fair hearing to all parties is essential to the manager's success. If at this stage he secures their support, his battle is two-thirds won. His hearing procedure is often more thorough than that of a court because he listens every day, learning from experience, whereas a court involves only a single case or controversy for only a stated period. | Trained as he is, the lawyer assumes all hearings need to be formal, as in a court of law. The longer they are the larger the fee he can justify. This is the root cause of the cost, delay, and inefficiency complained of by administrative-minded jurists such as Chief Justice Burger and other judicial reformers. They seek equivalent ways of dispensing justice, thus reducing the burden of courts. If administrators' equal rights were more widely respected, this needed reform would be greatly expedited. |

Because the court process starts at too early a stage—in the work of the so-called administrative law judges within the agencies themselves—the effect ultimately is to promote more litigation and more expense and delay than would otherwise be necessary. As a result, the courts and the system of justice as a whole are brought into citizen disrepute because of the overcongestion of dockets. In short, the invasion of the realm of professional administration is one of the main reasons that lawyers and the legal profession have been increasingly criticized by leading jurists as well as by the citizenry at large. By its nature, administrative justice at its best is more efficient than judicial justice.

SUBLEGISLATION

The lawyer, in his zeal, tries to reduce everything to "rule making," which is not realistically descriptive of what actually takes place. Increasingly, in recent years legislatures pass their most important legislation in skeleton form, stating the objectives and dealing with powers and organization, but leaving the interface of the law to administrative contrivance based upon policy, objectives, and administrative know-how. This is the only orderly way to run a government, as attested by foreign experience and the methods employed by large corporations.

Factor	Administrator	Lawyer
Concreteness	With one step logically leading to another, concretizing statutory intent is a must. As public policy is spelled out from constitution, to statute, to executive and administrative orders having the force of law, the administrator has the vehicle for everything he must do to pinpoint authority and responsibility.	In effect, the lawyer attempts to abrogate statutory intent by emphasizing rule instead of statute. The fight that he may have lost in the legislature is continued, and often with more success, in the prolonged hearings, delays, insistence upon inclusion of allied interests, and reviews, of proposed enforcement measures before they even go into operation. Much of the in-fighting would not be tolerated in a court of law. The fact that it has become so widespread and cumbersome attests to the constant encroachment of the legal profession upon the orderly and effective administration of government at all levels.
Standards	The administrator has always favored the term standards, because that is the way he is trained to think. He needs norms for everything he does. The standard not only	Since the Administrative Procedure Act of 1946, lawyers have lumped everything together under the rubric of rule making. Standards is an administrative term. The lawyers prefer to deduce

	assures equality of treatment but it also helps to make policy and objectives concrete.	authority from the common law instead of the statute, and hence they attempt to build a world consisting entirely of rules. Rules that they make and that they alone can understand.
Bill drafting	Bill drafting is an administrative matter of initiative, with final action by the legislature. Laws are no better than their administrative capability of enforcement. If bills were better drafted, much of what is now called rule making could be obviated.	Bill drafting is the monopoly of the legal profession. They are the experts on words and phrases. As long as the legalese is right, it matters not that the administrator and the citizen are frequently in doubt about what the legislation means. This makes more work for the lawyer and the judge.

Ernst Freund of the University of Chicago, who was the pioneer in bill-drafting reform, was clear about this. Make the law clear in the first place, and public policy execution will prosper and the red tape of lawyers and administrators will be reduced. When the legal profession drafts the statute, determines the rule making, and has a stranglehold on judicial decision within the administrative agency, the administrator, in effect, has his influence and expertise nullified. Lawyers should be advisers, what the administrator calls staff people. They should not be allowed to run the program.

Returning to my Immigration example, we had a committee on drafting legislation for immigration and naturalization in the Department of Justice, with the attorney-general being represented by someone from the solicitor-general's office. By agreement with the relevant committees of Congress, this committee consisting primarily of career executives, initiated all new legislation and amendments to existing laws coming from the Roosevelt administration, and was given the courtesy of considering all relevant legislation originating elsewhere, including that of members of Congress. The system worked very well. If every major program in government were similarly treated, a great improvement in government operations could be expected.

PROCEDURE

A word about procedure is necessary at this point because the administrative lawyer's obsession with procedure is a major source of irritation between the two professions.

Factor	Administrator	Lawyer
Inseparability	Substantive and procedural law are so closely intertwined that they are inseparable. Procedure is not an end in itself but something that grows out of policy and organization to achieve dynamic administration. To try to treat it as a detached entity only adds to bureaucratization.	Procedure is the sole concern of the practicing attorney and especially the trial lawyer. Know your procedure and you can commission experts to testify on substance. The acid test of a good law school is which does the best job of teaching procedure. Hence, by inference, the whole of administration is merely another courtroom.
Due process	Administrative due process is a must. Fairness and other aspects of due process become part of the administrator's philosophy. When he scrupulously adheres to them, he gains public cooperation and support, and hence it is in his self-interest.	Lawyers, being experts, have sole responsibility within action programs for enforcing administrative due process. They alone are experts on legal remedies, such as habeas corpus, injunction, and quo warranto.

In short, the administrator, no less than the lawyer, recognizes that adherence to due process is an integral part of his professional obligation. The administrator must be fair, avoid conflicts of interest, notify parties when hearings are held, provide for appeals to higher administrative authority as well as to the courts, keep a record of the reasons for his decisions as a matter of fairness and public accountability. None of this, within reasonable limits, is difficult to do, and administrators can easily master these requirements. It is a part of the day's work. If any administrator becomes careless, the courts can and should remind him of his responsibilities. But the courts should be outside, not inside, the flow of program enforcement.

The lawyers, in contrast, have sought and obtained for themselves a foothold within administrative agencies. This takes the form of hearing officers and administrative law judges who are autonomous, transferable, and who report not to the executive head of the program but to the Civil Service Commission or an independent professional board. The consequence is that the public business suffers from internal segmentation of what should be a unified programmatic management.

PERSONNEL MANAGEMENT

Personnel management, which should be the most dynamic element in administration, also has become increasingly judicialized and rendered bureaucratic and ineffectual since shortly after the time the Administrative Procedure Act of 1946 was passed. Lawyers, alone, are not to blame for this, because the staff agencies that have been created to deal with examination, hiring, promotion, firing, and the like, have been judicialized by these same expert staffs. "Personnel rules and regulations, which originated as a defense against spoils . . . now result in as much inefficiency as they were designed to prevent," says Alan Campbell, who engineered President Carter's Civil Service Reform Act of 1978 and its reorganization scheme.[1] "The system is so encrusted that many managers feel it is almost impossible to manage effectively," he continues. It may take months to hire or fire employees. There are altogether too many lawyers and people who act like lawyers to enable executives to do a good job. Moreover, it is not merely the labor unions of government employees who should be made to bear the responsibility for this sad state of affairs: the lawyers and personnel experts who think like them are even more to blame.

In private corporations the philosophical doctrine is that personnel matters are an integral part of the line official's undivided responsibilities. The personnel director advises but has no "power over," no line authority. In government the reverse has come to be true. Control is emphasized by personnel units instead of motivation. It is a negative approach, not a positive and dynamic one. In such cases personnel management may do more harm than good.

The tendency toward judicialization is clearly seen in the stages through which personnel management, as a profession, has gone since the turn of the century. In the initial period the emphasis was on factorial analysis, that is, defining jobs and learning to measure time and motion according to the principles that Frederick Taylor, of scientific management fame, invented. In the second period, which ran from 1932–38, the crisis of the Great Depression produced a relaxation of controls and there was an influx of managers who were given clear mandates, free from outside domination. This was a period when the practice more nearly resembled that of private industry than at any time since. This was also the period of highest governmental productivity. Then in the third period, commencing in 1938, departmental personnel chiefs were created for the first time, by congressional legislation, and the system worked well until the early 1950s. During the fourth period, which mirrored the influence of the lawyer's domination, the system has become progressively worse, leading to Campbell's caustic remarks.

The trouble, as Campbell was quoted as saying earlier, is rules, rules, rules, and more rules. The administrators had their hands tied.

When one searches for the reasons for excessive bureaucracy, the explanation is to be found in the unholy alliance of lawyers and personnel experts who think and act like lawyers. Personnel management, as a distinct profession, has got off the track. If it is to be useful and respected again, it must focus on releasing people's energies and giving them a challenge and a clear mandate. More psychologists and fewer lawyers are needed in personnel agencies.

Summarizing the eight areas of administration considered in this chapter, it has been seen that the administrator thinks that objectives are social, concrete, and related to a time period, while the lawyer focuses on the symmetry of the law. Second, the administrator wishes organization to be functional and flexible, whereas the lawyer seeks perfection and rigidity. Third, the administrator plans only what needs planning, whereas the lawyer's whole training and instinct is to make paper plans. Fourth, the administrator uses control mechanisms for information and evaluation, the lawyer for top-side dominance. Fifth, the administrator views decision as part of the flow of his ongoing work, the lawyer as an excuse to hold a formal hearing and make a fee. Sixth, the administrator regards sublegislation as part of an evolutionary scheme in which he progressively becomes more concrete; the lawyer, in contrast, regards decision as a judicial, not an administrative function, and tries to isolate it and dominate it. Seventh, the administrator refuses to isolate substance and procedure and believes that the latter grows out of the former, whereas the lawyer exhibits the same tendency he does when thinking about planning and regards procedure as mere protocol or paperwork. Finally, the administrator regards the human factor as his main reliance for dynamism and results, and refuses to turn this area over to others; the lawyer equates humans to robots and assumes that if they are provided with enough rules the system will be controlled, if nothing else.

The curious thing about this whole business, globally speaking, is that the Soviets started out with the idea that rules are efficient and gradually have learned that motivation is more important. The United States, on the other hand, started out with a free and independent spirit and increasingly has become a rule-ridden polity. Perhaps this is the time to see things in a clearer perspective.

NOTE

1. Alan Campbell, "Civil Service Reform: A New Commitment," *Public Administration Review* (March-April 1978): 100.

— 7 —

WHERE ADMINISTRATIVE LAW GOT OFF THE TRACK

Up to this point, the focus of this book has been almost entirely on the governmental, or institutional, application of public administration and administrative law. However, attention now will be turned to the academic setting where the teaching, research, and book and article writing take place, and where both lawyers and administrators get their mental set. Before one can hope to reform the application, one needs to go back to the origin of manpower supply and improve scholarly understanding and cooperation.[1]

In the United States, the divorcement of the public administration offering in arts and sciences faculties and the teaching of administrative law in law schools was apparent by 1940, but the trend started in the 1920s. Fortunately, the divorcement has never been complete, because there are still scholars in both faculties who have tried valiantly to hold the two strands together, realizing that their complete separation represents not merely a tilt but a distortion, with serious social consequences.

In historical perspective, three main periods may be distinguished in the United States. Between 1880 and 1923, both subjects were unified because they grew out of the same source, the administrative law of the Continent and the early political science of England. Between 1923 and 1940, the two subjects tended to differentiate more clearly but were still effectively collaborating within political science and law school faculties. The stimulus to the eventual separation occurred when, in a series of lectures on *The Growth of American*

Administrative Law sponsored by the American Bar Association, administrative law was defined as "a convenient term to indicate that branch of modern law relating to the executive department *when acting in a quasi-legislative or quasi-judicial capacity.*" In the final period from 1940 to the present, the two fields have grown steadily apart, as political science and public administration neglected law, and as law school courses on administrative law stopped teaching administration and concentrated on private rights, or regulation. It was in the 1940s, therefore, that the two subjects finally got off the track.

The significance of these developments may be assessed more clearly when it is realized that in continental countries and wherever the Roman law tradition prevails today, the two subjects have been continuously taught in the same faculty since the early part of the nineteenth century. Only recently, as in France and Germany, has the operational or functional approach to public administration (which is characterized as "American") begun to receive separate treatment in separate courses or training programs for future officials. In England, due largely to the influence of the London School of Economics and Political Science, administrative law and public administration, as distinct courses, arrived much later on the scene in the 1930s, and with wider emphasis only since the end of World War II.

It is not too much to say, therefore, that both administrative law and public administration, as academic subjects in the United States, received their original impetus from the Continent, where the attempt was to teach the whole of administration in a single course, and where treatises on administrative law sometimes run to seven or more volumes by the same author. Since historically this is the origin, perhaps the best way of appraising the integrated scope of public administration and administrative law is to consider the way continental scholars have developed their subject.

If one were starting afresh, there are five distinct but interrelated components of administration that would logically emerge: substantive, operational, agency, ruling case, and private rights and remedies.

STATE ACTIVITY

This is the substantive knowledge of functional fields. Examples of this are police, taxation, public works, and so on, an expanding list of subjects that increases as governments at all levels expand their scope. For the U.S. lawyer, the usual source of such information is the

United States Code Annotated (USCA), under rubrics similar to those mentioned above. For the U.S. public administrator, courses are sometimes taught on police, fire, public works, and similar subjects; generally, at the strictly academic level, public administration confines itself to what is universal, such as organization, personnel, and the subjects developed in Chapter 6 of this book.

Hence it is fair to say that in the United States, the substantive knowledge of the "what" of administration is widely dispersed throughout the university curriculum instead of being reassembled in a single faculty.

This is significant because if the substantive knowledge were brought together more frequently, the administrator receiving such intelligence early in his career presumably would be in a better position to develop policy, plans, and solutions than if this part of his training were neglected. In the law school domain, the professors who have made the greatest attempt to arouse interest in this subject—from my personal knowledge—were Felix Frankfurter, Walter Gellhorn, Ralph Fuchs, and Nathaniel Nathanson.

INTERNAL METHOD

This is knowledge of what the administrator and his staff do. It is the "how" of administration. Most of what is taught as public administration in the United States deals with this functional (operating) area. Its equivalent in law schools is called procedure, although, as has been seen, the bias is toward what the courts do rather than what the administrator does.

AGENCY LAW

By this is meant the law that the administrative agencies themselves make. In bulk, this record of policy, sublegislation, quasi-judicial decision, and internal rules of proceeding and due process exceeds by a ratio of hundreds to one the court cases that are the familiar diet of administrative law courses. This is distinguished from what was discussed under state activity, because although they are both agency (or operating) matters, the former deals with the science, art, and philosophy of an academic subject such as engineering, whereas agency law is what that term implies: the policies and decisions that have the force of law so far as the citizen is concerned.

One form this knowledge takes is the history of a case from the time an administrative agency gets hold of it to a decision in the particular case before the agency, and thence, as in a rate case of a public utility or a railroad case of the Interstate Commerce Commission, to the court decision in a state, or to the hierarchy of federal courts, district, appeals courts, and the Supreme Court of the United States.

Felix Frankfurter used to employ this method very effectively in his administrative law course at Harvard. In political science, Avery Leiserson shows how it is done in his book *Administrative Regulation* (1942), as does J. Roland Pennock in *Administration and the Rule of Law* (1941), and Pendleton Herring in *Public Administration and the Public Interest* (1936). Walter Gellhorn, in the 1940 edition of his *Administrative Law: Cases and Comments*, states that this is the way that administrative law ideally should be taught (p. 9), and I agree with him. I. L. Sharfman's four-volume work *The Interstate Commerce Commission* (1931–37), or, earlier, E. W. Patterson's *The Insurance Commissioner* (1927), both done under the aegis of The Twentieth Century Fund, are excellent historical studies of this kind.

LEADING COURT DECISIONS

This takes the form of casebooks on administrative law, which is the common vehicle for teaching administrative law in the United States. Ernst Freund, who was a political science student of Frank J. Goodnow at Columbia, published his *Cases on Administrative Law* as early as 1911, his second edition in 1928. Five years earlier than Freund, in 1906, Goodnow brought out his *Selected Cases on Administrative Law*, stressing the law of officers and the extraordinary remedies. The last of the casebooks by a political scientist was authored by Goodnow's colleague at Johns Hopkins, James Hart, and was called *An Introduction to Administrative Law with Selected Cases*, the first edition appearing in 1940 and the second in 1950.

Among the law school casebooks, Frankfurter's and Davison's *Cases and Other Materials on Administrative Law* appeared in 1932, foreshadowing the direction that law school teaching in this field was to take. In 1928 a colleague of Freund's at Chicago, Kenneth C. Sears, published *Cases and Materials on Administrative Law*. This was followed six years later by E. Blythe Stason's *The Law of Administrative Tribunals*, representing still further the drift away from administration in a broad sense and reflecting a preoccupation with major economic regulation. Walter Gellhorn's casebook came out in 1940, and although he expressed concern with the narrowing of the treatment of his subject in law schools, Gellhorn was forced to circumscribe his coverage appreciably, although it still showed the effect of the political science orientation of Goodnow in his Columbia days.

Of all the writers on administrative law in recent years, Kenneth C. Davis of Minnesota and the University of Chicago has been the most prolific and the most influential. His comprehensive treatise *Administrative Law* and his *Casebook* were both published in 1951. By 1958 he had completed a four-volume work, *Administrative Law Treatise*, followed a year later by *Administrative Law Cases*. Davis, who had been active in the work of the Attorney-General's Committee on Administrative Procedure, which reported in 1940, had come to have a feel for the problems of the practical administrator and suggested to the present author a book attempting to combine the fields of public administration and administrative law. Because of textbook commitments I was forced to honor, this book was never written, although the contract with West Publishing Company had been signed. Consequently, in 1960 Davis brought out a book called *Administrative Law and Government*, explaining in his preface that although the book is intended for liberal arts students it is, in effect, a condensation of his *Treatise* and hence follows the same outline. This 500-page book is divided into 30 chapters and deals, generally, with the administrative process, delegation of power, investigation, informal adjudicating, rule making, bias, separation of functions, evidence, official notice, findings, stare decisis, primary jurisdiction, exhaustion of administrative remedies, ripeness for review, tort and officer liability, and review of administrative findings.

Davis's textbook for liberal arts students is a useful book for future administrators and stresses things they need to know and ordinarily would not learn in a course on public administration. It does not deal exclusively with administrative procedure and it does deal with tort, governmental and officer liability, and some aspects of administrative due process. However, if one compares Davis's outline with the eight elements of administration dealt with in Chapter 6 of the present book, some prominent omissions will be detected, especially objectives, organization, planning, control as measurement, and personnel management. Putting it another way, the main areas of overlap between Davis's outline and this author's eight points is when he deals with rule making, decision making, and procedure. This, as suggested earlier, is in effect the main emphasis in the law school teaching of administrative law today.

PRIVATE RIGHTS AND REMEDIES

This subject is the one given the most attention in the law school approach, especially by writers such as Bernard Schwartz, who represents its apogee. It is not possible to assign an exact date to the development of this emphasis in law school orientation. Ernst Freund was certainly one of the first. His *Administrative Powers over Persons and Property*, published in 1928, four years before his death, is not only a classic, but it also doubtless had much to do with the shifting of emphasis from the public side to the private interest side of administration. Although Freund had a continental background and considered Goodnow the grand père of administration and himself, the petit père, he began to feel that administrative law, in the continental tradition and as taught by Goodnow, was not giving enough attention to private rights.[2] Goodnow was concerned with such things as organization and personnel, which was the continental tradition, and Freund was not.

"Goodnow viewed administrative law from the standpoint of the State," said Arthur T. Vanderbilt, "while Freund on the other hand was concerned primarily with the effect of administrative action on private right."[3] Vanderbilt was the conservative dean of the New York University Law School and always felt highly competitive toward academic political science. He wrote just one year before the American Bar Association staged its first triumph, in the form of the Walter-Logan Bill, curbing administrative power. So Freund's 1928 book was doubtless a vital turning point in the shifting of direction that law school administrative law was later to take.

Allied to private rights is the question of what Goodnow always called the "extraordinary" legal remedies. These common law writs such as mandamus injunction, and habeas corpus were developed by the courts to deal with a number of situations that affect the right of the individual to the redress of wrongs or the protection of his legal rights. In effect, they are sanctions, bringing parties into court, having them released from custody, or ordering certain things to be done or discontinued. They are in some cases the inherent power courts have to enforce their authority, and in such cases are widely used. In at least one instance, however, quo warranto (with what warrant), the writ is nowadays used very infrequently to test the right to public office.

The main problem, however, remains. That is to assure the judiciary's protection of the individual against nonfeasance, misfeasance, and generally an abuse of power. This aspect of administrative law is even more greatly emphasized in continental countries. The existence of a separate but parallel system of administrative courts alongside the private, civil law ones is evidence of this fact. The development was speeded up particularly after the Napoleonic period of the early nineteenth century, following the French Revolution of 1789. The continental countries, and especially France, have done a good job of it. What the French call excès du pouvoir is one of the main objectives of this form of administrative justice. No official can claim power simply because he is an official, but must show legal justification for his claimed authority or the way he exercises it. The other distinctive doctrine is governmental responsibility for torts. The principal (the political state) should be held responsible in damages for the unlawful acts of its agents. This goes beyond what has been attained in Anglo-American law, though much work has been done on this in recent years.

The five main areas initially suggested as the grand edifice of administrative action from which an integrated fusion of public administration and administrative law might conceivably emerge have been covered. These five are the substantive field of state function and activity (the what); the internal method of administering (the how); the law that the individual agencies make (the sublegisla-tion and quasi-judicial powers); the case law made by the courts (the law); and, finally, the protection of individual rights and the supplying of remedies to guarantee these rights (personal rights).

If training along these lines for both public administrators and lawyers could be developed, both professional fields, law and public administration, would clearly receive considerable benefit, as would the nation as a whole.

Public administration, like law, suffers from too little attention to the substance of public policy and the professional know-how of its several fields. The Soviets, in contrast, have in the neighborhood of 2,000 institutes, like those for steel and nuclear science. In each of these, management is taught with varying degrees of emphasis to everyone, which is no mean advantage. Obviously there is a prima facie case for maintaining an open mind concerning possible new combinations of materials for use in U.S. teaching institutions.

Since there is some disagreement about the history of adminis-trative law in the United States, with some occasionally claiming that it is a twentieth-century invention, and since a knowledge of authors is desirable, what follows is a general sequence of scholarly effort in the United States to date.

SOME STEPS IN THE EVOLUTION OF ADMINISTRATIVE
LAW AND PUBLIC ADMINISTRATION

In 1886 Frank J. Goodnow wrote an article on "Judicial Remedies against Administrative Actions" in volume one of Columbia's *Political Science Quarterly*. He noted that there were already certain books in existence that form a part of administrative law: Dillon's *Law of Municipal Corporations*, (1872), and Cooley's *Law of Taxation* (1876). In 1890 Mechem's *Law of Officers* appeared. In 1887, a year after Goodnow's article was published, Woodrow Wilson's famous essay, "A Study of Administration," was published in volume two of the *Political Science Quarterly*. This article of Wilson's in which he describes public administration by analogy to business, marked the real beginning of public administration in the United States, and gave it its orientation.

The acknowledged father of administrative law, Goodnow published *Comparative Administrative Law* in 1893, *Politics and Administration*, which represented an initial attempt to combine the two fields, in 1900, and *The Principles of the Administrative Law of the United States* in 1905. Goodnow also was interested in municipal government and social legislation and wrote *Municipal Home Rule*, *Municipal Problems*, *Municipal Government*, and *Social Reform and the Constitution*.

Another pioneer, W. F. Willoughby, was both public lawyer and the earliest sustained writer in the field of public administration. He was for many years director of governmental studies at the Brookings Institution in Washington, D.C. As early as 1891 he coauthored with his brother, W. W. Willoughby, *Government and Administration in the United States*. However, his main distinction is his trilogy, *Principles of Public Administration* (1927), *Principles of Judicial Administration* (1929), and *Principles of Legislative Organization and Administration* (1934). Not only is Willoughby the only author who has written definitive books on the administration of all three branches in the United States, but he also is justly famous for inventing the idea that there is a legitimate fourth branch of government, the administrative, which is properly distinguished from the executive and reports to both Congress, as board of directors, and to the president, as chief executive.

In 1926 Leonard D. White of the University of Chicago published *An Introduction to Public Administration*, which became the first textbook in this field. His primary emphasis was upon personnel explain the social milieu. The special reason is that in the United States, regulation as a device of social control is utilized to a far greater extent than it is in other countries. Where other countries create a state enterprise for railroads, telephones, and other forms of public utility, U.S. preference since about 1887 has been for regulation of specially chartered companies. There are a dozen or more of these major regulatory agencies in Washington and the number grows all the time, the Nuclear Regulatory Agency being one of the latest. Since they deal with the stock exchange, the enforcement of the antitrust laws, the various forms of energy (such as electricity), with transportation in all its forms, food and drug, environment, and the like, they are concerned with the very heart of the capitalist system. One group of officials, usually in the form of a board or commission, is set up to charter, set prices and determine allowable rates of return, determine standards of service, decide on mergers and discontinuances—in short, deal with all important areas of administration that the regulated industry is concerned with. This even applies to such things as the kind of accounting system it must maintain, how much may be spent on advertising, and other questions that are traditionally considered matters of internal management.

So powerful and important are these regulatory agencies, and so much legal business results from their activities, that it is not surprising that gradually administrative law, as taught in the law schools, has come increasingly to concentrate primarily, or even almost exclusively, on this segment of industry and government. It is in such areas that the Washington law firms make their largest fees. Green mentions almost $500,000 charged a large natural gas company, and fees ranging from $211,000 to $524,000 charged to three airlines for single cases (p. 9).

Hence the cause-and-effect relationship: the more areas that government regulates and the larger the interests of private companies that are at stake, the more interest the law firms take in them. Also, the greater is the tendency to stress these areas in law schools so long as the basic assumption is that everything is private law.

It is an easy rationalization to state that since independent regulatory commissions make decisions, they should be treated more like courts than like ordinary administrative departments and bureaus. Then it is the next logical step to argue that since commissions that regulate the infrastructure already have been judicialized, other forms of regulation should be similarly judicialized. Third, since government increasingly regulates "new" areas of public life, the lawyer seeks to extend his control over them as well. Finally, as management, but being both a student and colleague of Ernst Freund, he was interested in administrative law and shared Freund's orientation. He later distinguished himself by writing several good books on government career service and was a member of the United States Civil Service Commission during the Roosevelt administration.

In addition to the other books of Ernst Freund that already have been noted, prominent consideration should be given to his scholarship in the field of legislation, where he was a pioneer: *Legislative Drafting* (1916), *Standards of Legislation* (1917), and *Legislative Regulation: A Study of the Ways and Means of Written Law* (1932). He also is justly famous for his interest in aliens and the Chicago School of Social Work, plus several monographs dealing with labor law. Freund also was a prime mover in the uniform state law movement. In addition, he was a pioneer in the study of police power, as exemplified by his book, *The Police Power: Public Policy and Constitutional Rights* (1904). This early book doubtless had something to do with his espousal of private rights in his 1928 book, *Administrative Powers over Persons and Property.*

Felix Frankfurter not only wrote one of the earliest casebooks on administrative law, but he also had a lifelong interest in practical administration, having served in Washington around the time of World War I. This practical experience is reflected in books such as *The Business of the Supreme Court* (with James M. Landis, 1928), *The Labor Injunction* (with Nathan Greene, 1930), *The Public and Its Government* (1930), *Mr. Justice Holmes* (1931), *Cases on Federal Jurisdiction* (with Wilber G. Katz, 1931), and *Mr. Justice Brandeis* (1932). It is possible that Frankfurter early had a better understanding of practical administration than any other law school writer of books on administrative law.

Another pioneer, Roscoe Pound, also was close to the interests of political scientists and public administrators all his life. He was essentially a philosopher and statesman of the law, but his interest in administration was intense. Among his many books the following are especially relevant: *Outlines of Lectures on Jurisprudence* (1914), *The Spirit of the Common Law* (1921), *An Introduction to the Philosophy of Law* (1922), *Law and Morals* (1924), *Criminal Justice in America* (1930), and *Administrative Law: Its Growth, Procedure and Significance* (1942).

During the 1920s and 1930s a number of political scientists exercised a considerable influence in the field of administrative law: James Hart, *Ordinance Making Power of the President* (1925); J. P. Comer, *Legislative Functions of National Administrative Authorities* (1927); John Dickinson, *Administrative Justice and the Supremacy of*

Law (1927); W. C. Van Vleck, *The Administrative Control of Aliens* (1932); Frederick E. Blachly and Miriam E. Oatman, *Administrative Legislation and Adjudication* (1934); and J. P. Chamberlain et al., *The Judicial Function in Federal Administrative Agencies* (1942).

Because of their impact on U.S. thinking, a number of books by English authors also should be mentioned: Robert Carr, *Delegated Legislation* (1921); William A. Robson, *Justice and Administrative Law* (1928); F. J. Port, *Administrative Law* (1929); and Lord Hewart's polemic, *The New Despotism* (1929).

Another U.S. political scientist who has distinguished himself equally in law and administration is J. Roland Pennock. His earliest book, *Administration and the Rule of Law* (1941), is something of a classic. Because of his deep insights into legal philosophy, two more recent books of Pennock are equally rewarding (both with John W. Chapman): *The Limits of Law* (1974) and *Due Process* (1977). Pennock is one of those rare spirits who throughout a long professional life has helped to keep law and administration congenially inter-twined.

The present author is another U.S. political scientist who always has kept one foot in administrative law and the other in public administration. Following the appearance of his *Congressional Investigating Committees* (1929), he edited (with C. G. Haines) *The Law and Practice of Administration* (1935); published *The Frontiers of Public Administration* (with Gaus and White, 1936), *Modern Politics and Administration* (1937), *The Immigration and Naturalization Service* (with Henry M. Hart, Jr. and John McIntire, 1940), four editions of *Public Administration* (with Gladys Ogden Dimock), the first in 1953, *A Philosophy of Administration* (1958), and *Casebook in Public Administration* (joint author, 1969). His early articles on administrative law, reflecting Goodnow's influence, whose student he was, are found in *Public Administration* (London, 1931), *American Political Science Review* (1932), and various other publications.

Among those law school professors who have been mentioned earlier, Walter Gellhorn has continued his interest in discovering alternative ways to formal courts of law for dispensing justice. This is reflected in two of his recent books, *Ombudsmen and Other Citizens' Protectors in Nine Countries* (1966), and *When Americans Complain: Governmental Grievance Procedures* (1966). Of all the law school professors active today, Gellhorn probably has a better appreciation of the virtue of interdisciplinary solidarity than anyone else.

Bernard Schwartz of New York University is, like Kenneth Davis, another prolific author. In addition to his 1976 *Administrative Law*, which has been cited often, his book entitled *The Professor and the*

Commissions (1959), will be found interesting, and his book written with H. W. R. Wade, *Legal Control of Government: Administrative Law in Britain and the United States* (1972), presents some interesting contrasts.

I realize that in this brief review I have neglected significant authors such as Louis Jaffe, Ralph Fuchs, Nathaniel Nathanson, and many others, some of whom are close friends. Yet I beg forgiveness because my object has been quite limited: to convey some impression of the stages through which joint scholarship has gone and the degree to which authors from the two fields have either interlaced or gone their separate ways. I hope even this brief historical résumé has contributed something to an understanding of the historical integration of the two fields.

What is one to conclude from this chapter's survey of 100 years of courtship and alienation? The first thing is that administrative law is by no means a twentieth-century invention. It had a long history on the Continent before it was transplanted over here. At the outset the partners enjoyed connubial bliss because both came out of the legal-juristic tradition: political science was law and law was political science. Both were subdivisions under their patron saint, philosophy. There was no special merit in being called a lawyer or a political scientist. Political science was a point of view: comparative, analytical, believing in first principles, willing to experiment, not averse to turning its attention to municipal corruption, the exploitation of aliens, labor relations, or Sacco and Vanzetti, as Felix Frankfurter did in his first book.

Even as late as 1938, as I can recall from personal experience, lawyers and political scientists seemed unaware of any hereditary differences. Roscoe Pound courted Charles Grove Haines to go to Harvard Law School and give his lectures on the revival of natural law concepts; Edward S. Corwin of Princeton was, in both fields, the acknowledged expert on the presidency; lawyers pored over W. W. Willoughby's four volumes on constitutional law and marveled at the breadth of his scholarship and the accuracy of his interpretations; when I went to Chicago in 1932, one of the inducements held out to me was that Freund and I both were students of Frank J. Goodnow and Freund was about to retire (he died the same year).

Unlike now, neither side hesitated to quote the other profession as readily as its own. All this is now changed. One may read an entire book on administrative law and never find a reference to any of those works dealt with in the above historical summary. But this, unfortunately, is true today of most professional fields, with the possible exceptions of sociology and philosophy, which are considered mavericks.

But as has been seen, there have been throughout some who refused to budge from their fealty to a common citizenship. Frankfurter and Gellhorn are good examples in law, Haines and Pennock in political science. Another like this was Oliver P. Field of the University of Minnesota. The impression is that there were giants abroad in former times, men in both law and political science who were big enough to rise above any petty personal, professional, or scholastic rivalries.

One naturally wonders whether the accelerated drawing apart that began to occur in 1940 was due to differences in conservative or liberal philosophy. Perhaps in a few cases, but not in many. Most of those mentioned, such as Frankfurter, Goodnow, and Freund, were conservative in some things, liberal in others. Pound was that way, too. Some have suspected that as he got older he became more conservative, some would say ultraconservative; but if one reads his Claremont lectures, which is one of the last things he did, that impression is rapidly dispelled. His theme still was change and adjusting to change, but he continued to seek values in law and political philosophy that were congruent.

In terms of understanding the history of ideas, it was the New Deal, not so much the individual philosophies of scholars, that tended to create polarities. New agencies were being established at a rapid rate, as I learned from the vantage point of assistant secretary of Labor in charge of legislation and administration. Lawyers understandably felt that administrative justice might, if the trend was not checked, overwhelm the traditional common law. Perhaps, in their concern, some individuals and the legal profession as a whole overreacted. In hindsight, it seems to this observer that they did. But as Aristotle pointed out long ago, this excessive zeal still can be righted, because the pendulum always has swung from one extreme to another, in short time cycles, and seldom, if ever, stands still.

The problem now is that of correctly appraising the requirements of the period that appears to lie ahead. In this period, as Mr. Justice Scarman said in his lectures, English Law—The New Dimension (1975), problems such as the European Community, the rival claims of organized labor and management, and the whole complex of social welfare cannot help but challenge the best thought of both professional disciplines, working together on solutions. The central problem is still, as it was in 1890 when Mechem wrote, a matter of political philosophy in its deepest sense. Society is an interconnected organism and hardly any problem can be dealt with adequately in splendid isolation. Pound and Goodnow were both clear about this in their heyday. Philosophers still believe that this is true, as seen in such seminal works as Summers' *Essays in Legal Philosophy* (1976) and Ronald Dworkin's *Taking Rights Seriously* (1977), which are attempting to revitalize this idea.

The field of law and administration needs big men with wide and deep insights and a charitable attitude toward cousins and second cousins. Future lawyers and administrators can develop this intimate knowledge of each other's fields simply by reading a few well-selected books. The case method should continue to be utilized in the preparation of both sets of experts, but it should not be used exclusively. Public lawyers and public administrators both can combine private and public interest without neglecting either. Perhaps the necessary first step in accomplishing this adjustment is to take a hard look at the preconceptions of one's academic field, as Dwight Waldo did in *The Administrative State* (1948), and more recently in *The Study of Public Administration* (1955).

One need not reject the past to build the future. The past is needed, with appropriate innovations, to assure the kind of future that measures up to the attainments of the past.

NOTES

1. The best single historical and analytical examination of this subject was written by John A. Fairlie of the University of Illinois, under the title, "Public Administration and Administrative Law," in *Essays on the Law and Practice of Governmental Administration*, ed. Charles G. Haines and Marshall E. Dimock (Baltimore: Johns Hopkins University Press, 1935), pp. 3–43.

2. Oscar Kraines, *The World and Ideas of Ernst Freund: The Search for General Principles of Legislation and Administrative Law* (University, Ala.: University of Alabama Press, 1974), Introduction.

3. Arthur T. Vanderbilt, "One Hundred Years of Administrative Law," in *Law: A Century of Progress* (New York: New York University Press, 1937), p. 121.

— *PART TWO* —

SOME PROBLEM AREAS REQUIRING RESOLUTION

— 8 —

MAKING THE LAWS

In any attempt to improve the quality of administrative justice in Anglo-American countries, the obvious starting place is in the legislature, where bills are introduced and statutes are enacted. If the language of statutes were clearer, the administrator's responsibility for quasi-legislation and decision making would become clearer, and in consequence there would be less provocation than there has been since 1938 for the organized bar to interfere so much. Powerful interests would still doubtless attempt to neutralize administration for their own selfish ends, but the American Bar Association and the general public would be in a stronger position to exercise restraint and judgment.

Before this change can take place, it seems clear that communications between the legal and the public administration professions, and between them and the public, need to be improved. This is no easy thing, because, as sociologists and the Marshall McLuhans are constantly saying, the more professionalized a group becomes, the more pronounced its tendency to talk only to itself. Even Ernst Freund, who is acknowledged to be the greatest authority on legislation the United States has produced, exhibits this trait to a marked degree.

Freund thought of law in the real sense as "the rational ordering of human affairs."[1] From this initial assumption, he developed a dualism: the rational or declaratory law is the law establishing private rights that center in the common law and the decisions of the judiciary—without the intervention of legislatures or administrative agencies of any kind. He does not use the term, but this kind of law might be called pure law. The other kind of law Freund calls regulative law. It has a lower status than real law and it has a twofold purpose: to deal with the organization and powers of the legislative and administrative branches—what might be called the housekeeping functions or the public law—and second, to modify (subject to court approval) the rights of individuals as acted upon by the legislative and administrative branches.

In his book *Legislative Regulation* (1932), which was the most mature expression of his views, Freund signifies this intention clearly, for example, in calling Part I, "Legislation as a form of law." In other words, statutory law affects private interest merely indirectly, as it organizes the powers of the legislature and the administrative services. This idea, as has been seen in an earlier chapter, also survives in Britain today, as illustrated by the books of Mr. Justice Scarman and Nevil Johnson. Freund's basic dichotomy is complicated still further because he classifies all functions of government as service, which he applauds, and regulative, which he looks upon with suspicion because of their potentiality for interfering with private rights.

The complication is added to still further because of the broad way in which he uses the term regulative. In other words, unlike Frankfurter, Schwartz, and more recent authors in administrative law, he does not refer merely to major regulation, such as is exhibited in the independent regulatory commissions since the Interstate Commerce Commission was created in 1887, but includes any form of legislation that affects the private rights of individuals in any and all areas of legislation.

His explanation of this dichotomy between declaratory and regulative law is that his approach is juristic. He is talking only to lawyers, who are concerned with the majesty of law in the real sense.

Freund undoubtedly was correct in using the term regulative in the broad sense he did, and if others used it that way it would greatly clarify the issues dealt with in this book. All legislation is broadly regulative of human rights and obligations, and hence it is logically wrong to single out arbitrarily certain areas of governmental legislation and argue that they are essentially judicial instead of administrative. Logically, it is a matter of degree, not a difference in kind.

But it is wrong to assume that law making by legislatures is of a different and lower kind than real law, because this would cast doubt on the underlying assumptions of constitutional government and in effect reject the idea of popular government. The problem of legislation is not that it is of a lower order, but that it could and should be improved so as to assure greater fairness and effectiveness and a better ordering of public life in terms of a country's values.

In what he calls "the Hierarchy of Law in the United States," Harvey Walker in *Law Making in the United States* (1934) sets forth what is clearly the correct view of U.S. constitutional law as follows:

Federal: The Constitution of the United States, as interpreted by the Supreme Court

Acts of Congress

Treaties

Rules and ordinances made by the president and the executive department and by the federal courts

State: State constitutions, as interpreted by the several state supreme courts

Laws, made jointly by the state legislatures and the state executives

Rules and ordinances made by the governor or by the state executive departments or by the state courts

The common law—made by the courts

Municipal ordinances—made by municipal councils

He then explains, "each type takes precedence, in case of conflict, over all those shown below it. Acts of Congress and treaties stand on a place of equality. The one latest in point of time governs in case of conflict" (p. 2).

If lawyers had a greater respect for legislative-made law, perhaps they would focus more of their energy on improving the legislative branch of government and not make administration their whipping boy. Equally, if administrators did not regard bar associations primarily as pressure groups and still could look upon them as champions of popular government, as once they could, perhaps they would have a higher regard for lawyers and the law. Hence prospective administrators would be more inclined to study law as part of their professional preparation, something they seem to have been averse to since Charles A. Beard complained about "the tyranny of lawyers" in the 1930s.

Perhaps Freund was unwittingly influenced by three factors that distorted his views of law making in the United States. First, he said time and time again that law making in the United States is greatly inferior to law making in Europe, where he originated; second, his admiration of the doctrine of judicial supremacy undoubtedly colored his attitude toward the other two branches, as it does the attitude of most lawyers; and third, he was concerned with the protection of private rights in the United States because he came from a part of the world, where, even in the nineteenth century, monarchies and dictatorships still had considerably less tenderness for civil liberties than is found in the U.S. Bill of Rights.

If the improvement of legislation is as important as has been argued, it might be useful to refer in passing to some of the common grounds of citizen discontent. Several shall be mentioned, but not all developed, because the subject is almost so large as to be unmanageable. There are too many laws; too much of life is regulated, and needlessly so; the cost of government is consequently excessive; in comparison with other countries, U.S. legislatures are so plodding that they cannot guarantee acting in time even when it is essential that they should do so, as in an oil embargo or a runaway inflation; there are too many partisan political decisions and not enough statesmanship centering on the good of the country and the extended welfare of the people; legislatures do not have a sense of priorities and in consequence the making of law is overshadowed by other activities, such as being errand boy to constituents, and junketing; the staffing of Congress, which was virtually nonexistent in 1946, is now excessive; the legislative and executive branches spend too much time fighting each other and not enough time solving problems and going home; and it is almost hopeless to try to pin responsibility for acting or failing to act on institutions or individuals because there is no such thing as party responsibility. The problems are so numerous and in some instances so serious that the unfolding is almost enough to challenge the resourcefulness of the proverbial Philadelphia lawyer.

The suggestions that follow fall into two categories: those pertaining to the institution, and those internal matters designed to improve the quality of the product itself.

Congress needs to be reorganized for a second time. The first effort, which took the form of the Legislative Organization Act of 1946, was successful, but did not go far enough. As a member of the Committee on Congress of the American Political Science Association, I took an active part in that reorganization. Some of the things that need to be done now are these: the use of joint committees of both houses to consider important pieces of legislation. This would save time, especially when the country faces a crisis. The joint committee could be constituted much as committees of conference are now chosen. Second, there should be fewer committees and subcommittees of both houses and they should be geared to the organization of the executive branch so far as possible. Members wear themselves out attending committee meetings. Third, there should be joint planning of legislative timetables by the leaders of the Congress and the president and his closest Cabinet members working together. Finally, there should be a research agency on the national economy and natural resources, modeled much like the National Resources Planning Board, which existed between 1933 and 1943, to serve both the executive and legislative branches.

The second major institutional reform would aim at increasing the amount of responsibility in government. This has grown imperceptibly at both the national and state levels in recent years, but it does not go far enough. The principal form this takes is to differentiate more sharply between administration (party in power) bills and other bills. The precedent for this is the division of subject matter between government and private bill legislation as found in the British Parliament for generations. I know from being a state legislator that every conscientious legislator feels that he must introduce bills if he is to justify his existence. This instinct, plus the almost limitless scope of pressure group activity under our system, constitutes the basic reason for too much restrictive legislation. Lawmakers are continually looking for bills to attach their names to. If the amount of legislation were reduced—as it should be—and if more attention were given to administrative feasibility and cost, the chief complaint of the taxpayer that government does too much could be largely obviated.

This is not said in a conservative spirit. It is a hardheaded approach to better government. For when government attempts to do too much it often winds up doing nothing really well. This should be accompanied by a move to decentralize everything to state and local jurisdictions that can be so decentralized without neglecting human values and fairness to all concerned. More of the total tax dollar should go to state and local governments and less should be dispensed by Washington officials as a result of direct enforcement.

Third, there should be consistency in the interpretation of the separation of powers. Under the U.S. frame of government, both Congress and the president are responsible for directing the administrative departments and agencies. Accordingly, Congress and its committees should deal with the heads of program administration face-to-face, as they once did, instead of dealing with presidential aides and higher policy officials who frequently lack first-hand familiarity with the law as being administered.

As long as Congress, under the Constitution, has the authority to create and abolish programs, determine the organization and powers of action agencies, and appropriate their funds, dealing directly with program managers is the only way that accountability can be enforced. If there were more face-to-face relationships of this kind, the amount of special investigation by committees of Congress could be reduced in favor of more orderly procedure.

If Congress' surveillance function were better formulated, there would be less excuse for attempting to move lawyers into the action programs as policy makers and judges, thus weakening the administrative enforcement of the law. My experience is that members of Congress are usually down-to-earth and knowledgeable about administration—partly, no doubt, because they are laymen. If their talents were used more effectively, the country could cut down on the number of its laws and get more return on dollar expenditure than is now true, as there is so much duplication and waste and programs are continued long after they have proved ineffectual.

Finally, there is a need for more inventiveness. Instead of passing another regulative law, sometimes the better policy is to make use of positive incentives in connection with laws already passed or to stimulate voluntary action. This is usually the realm of the social psychologist and not the lawyer. These possibilities should be studied by private associations and the research foundations, on a contract basis, if necessary. Instead of passing another law imposing more red tape on everyone, ways should be found of dealing with the small minority of chiselers who cause the complaint in the first place. In other words, it is the analogue of attempts to clear court dockets by discovering equivalent and substitute means of dealing with minor offenses through such devices as arbitration, small claims courts, masters, and the like. Something inventive such as this needs to be done instead of passing new legislation every time there is a 1 percent minority of chiselers. Alternative remedies might reduce somewhat the employment opportunities for both lawyers and administrators, but the service would be sharper, and the country more able to compete in world markets.

What the conservative lawyers who favor more and more rules for government do not seem to realize is the analogy to what has happened in the labor unions. An excess of rules on the part of labor unions has been largely responsible for causing British industry, and to a lesser degree U.S. industry, to decline in recent years. This is evident in the use of a dozen or more craft unions in a single operation while building ships, when one would produce superior results. The stratification and lack of cooperation between labor unions have become so great that German, then Greek, and now Japanese shipyards wind up taking over the business. What these same conservative lawyers do not seem to realize is that exactly the same consequences ensue when governmental administration becomes excessively stratified and jurisdictional.

The amount of legislation could be reduced if a system of responsible Cabinet government were installed. It is surprising, in a way, that this has not been done, because responsible government is what U.S. business represents, and at least since Herbert Hoover's time the United States has been called (and justly) "a businessman's civilization." If business did not have so low an opinion of government, a move to responsible government would have taken place long ago, probably during the 1920s. (Business has blocked such a development because it considers government a competitor and does not realize its indispensability if business itself is to survive.) In business it is the paid management that studies problems, comes up with solutions, submits them to the board of directors, and then carries out the program without interference. This is the way government should operate, too, and in time it will, out of sheer considerations of survival. A government that cannot move when it needs to do so is like a duck with a broken leg sitting on a pond. A responsible government also learns to say "no" when it needs to, because if it doesn't it will now be respected, and the voters will react at future elections. It is supposed that the memory of the average voter is short: I doubt this very much. When I talk to my neighbors about the Teapot Dome investigation of the 1920s, which was the subject of my first book, they often don't know it involved petroleum, but they do know it was like Watergate and that in both cases a Republican administration was in power.

The point is that when governments have the fortitude and strong sense of principle to say "no" to legislation or expenditures, voters admire such courage and give such leadership future support. Nevertheless, because the United States lacks the degree of coordination and control that is needed, the government often resembles a lady of easy virtue, and almost any interest can bend her to their will. Easy yielding must have been what Aristotle had in mind when he used the word corrupt to describe the extreme tendencies of pure democracy. Every government needs an establishment of sorts, even if it is nothing more than an assemblage of strong-minded men and women from all classes who are bound together by a sense of commitment to the country. Lawyers used to have this sense of noblesse oblige, but they began to lose it in the 1930s. Government needs a sense of noblesse oblige in a stabilizing position today.

Turning next to the internal improvements that need to be made in the law-making process, there are a number of concrete proposals that have been touched upon previously but that need to be further amplified.

The first has to do with the job description of the legislature in the enactment of statutes. It already has been suggested that Congress, like most legislatures, tries to do too much and as a result fails to concentrate on actual lawmaking as much as it should. Joseph P. Chamberlain, in *Legislative Processes, National and State* (1936), commences his treatment of this subject with what seems to this author to be the correct view: "The making of law does not imply that any legislature originates legislation. They are law-declaring rather than lawmaking." To the same effect is the view of George B. Galloway, who headed the committee that engineered the Legislative Organization Act of 1946. In his book, *The Legislative Process in Congress* (1953), Galloway states that "few bills are conceived out of the independent thought and judgment of the individual lawmaker. Very little legislation originates within the legislature itself" (p. 38). The executive branch formulates and executes, the legislature determines new policy and evaluates the performance of administration. The executive departments are the main source of new or amendatory legislation and Galloway is convinced that this is the way it should be.

There are three main kinds of statute law: first, creative or new law; second, amendments, supplements, and repeals; and third, revisions, codifications, consolidations, and compilations (Galloway, p. 48). There are eight parts of congressional statutes: title, table of contents, enacting clause, definition of terms, the main body of the law in numbered titles and sections, followed by exceptions, provisos and savings clauses, a separability clause (in case any part is held invalid), and finally a provision for effective dates of the several titles and sections (p. 51). When the administration is the chief source of legislation, the stages are usually as follows. Someone in the administration or in an allied interest group gets an idea for new legislation or amendments to the law. The idea is worked over and submitted to a member or members of the appropriate committee of Congress as sponsors; it is then cleared with the president's staff agency (formerly the Bureau of the Budget, now the Office of Management and Budget). Changes may be made by the legislative members or their committee before holding public hearings in which parties of interest are heard, usually starting with the representative for the executive branch. From this time on, the procedure may differ, depending upon the rules of the legislature, but there is always a debate, three readings and votes on the bill, following which, or synchronously, the same procedure takes place in the second chamber. Then, if there is a difference, a committee of conference may be appointed to iron out disagreements. It is a long and thorough treatment of the subject and should produce a desirable product.

Galloway states what is a common view, however:

> One of the most important aspects of lawmaking is careful drafts-manship. Yet the statute books of every American legislature show that the work of drafting has often been poorly performed. Many of the laws passed cannot be expected to mean what they say; some mean nothing; and others attempt to provide for utterly impossible things (p. 51).

These are strong words, and perhaps they are unduly pessimistic. Yet it was out of such convictions that Freund concluded early in his career that improved draftsmanship is the key to improved administrative performance and for reconciling the difference between the rival skills of the lawyer and the administrator. The way to prevent excessive sublegislation by administrators is to do a better job of legislative draftsmanship in the first place.

The key to this reconciliation is to give equal status to the administrator and the lawyer in the perfecting of legislation. At present, most of the drafting is done by lawyers alone. But the added expense is well worth the extra cost, because, as Galloway points out, if the statute is badly drawn there may be much expenditure and little concrete accomplishment. The reason for the double review is this: the administrator supplies practical experience concerning workability, which is the payoff, and second, he is able to judge whether the words and phrases are expressed in as simple and clear English as can be provided. The lawyer, on the other hand, is essential to the team effort because his main expertness is in matters of constitutionality, conflict with other statutes, and an informed guess as to what courts of law will do with various aspects of law once the statute runs the judicial gauntlet. It may be objected that since most legislation already originates with administrators, this should give them all the opportunity needed to make their input effective. Much painful experience points to the fact, however, that last-minute changes in words and phrases may inadvertently (sometimes consciously) render the administrative enforcement virtually impossible, and hence the double check is amply justified.

Turning to the second problem of draftsmanship, if clarity is so important, why not consolidate the statutory law and codify the entire body of law, as in European countries? Freund has some interesting things to say about both of these subjects in all of his books on legislation. On the whole, he was inclined to favor consolidation and codification, and this was one main reason for his thinking that European statutory law is superior to the Anglo-American (*Standards of American Legislation*, p. 287). In connection with this, he argued that the case-by-case method of the common law is an inadequate basis for formulating public policy (pp. 68-70). But if all law, statutory, jurisprudential, case, and whatnot, were divided by main topics into (say) a half-dozen codes, some dealing with civil law and others with criminal law or administrative law, then there could be little question as to whether the administrator was acting within the perimeters of his authority and discretion. If the legislature wanted the administrator to have discretion it would merely say so. In other words, Freund's idea of legal excellence was precision. He was not interested in rules, which is too limited a concept; his interest was in statutory law incorporated into codes that could be found in one place and with a high degree of certainty. Another reason consolidation of statutory law and codes of law appealed to Freund is that it enabled jurists, as well as judges and lawmakers, to work over the corpus of the law continually, leading to the expectation that constant, instead of intermittent, care would produce a superior product.

There has long been a strong objection to the European system of codification in both Britain and the United States. National pride has something to do with it. That is why Dicey castigated the whole idea of a separate administrative law and separate administrative courts, only to recant later in life to a considerable extent. Lack of knowledge is another factor. It is a complex explanation; even the reduced opportunities for making a living at legal practice possibly may creep in.

But the more serious objections are these: first, that it would be difficult to keep the codes current and adjusted to social change; second, that if the history of leaving laws on the statute books is any guide, the codes probably would remain in effect long after the time that they were thought effective; third, that in a country where the separation of powers is so much cherished, the legislature might be jealous and the Supreme Court might frown upon the upstart code; fourth, if the codes were not carefully drawn, the hands of administrators might be tied more tightly than they are at present, where administrators complain about insufficient discretion and restricted freedom to unify the flow of administration strategy; finally, in making the codification there would be an ideal opportunity for powerful interests to put "jokers" in the code that would not be detected right away. This frequently has been charged, for example, when state criminal codes were being considered by the legislature and liberals were agitated about intent or possible interpretation.

Despite all these objections, there has been a steady and apparently unremitting tendency toward consolidation of laws, as in immigration, and also for codifying the law by main segments, starting with the ones that are easiest and less debatable, such as contracts. But constitutional or administrative law? Especially those vague words such as "due process of law" or "fair and reasonable"? That would be a nightmare, indeed, and all except the intrepid would hesitate to undertake it. Similarly with police power, about which Freund wrote as early as 1904.

My conclusions regarding consolidation and codification are therefore as follows. Consolidation is frequently a good idea. When I was in Immigration, for example, we discovered that seven separate statutes dealt with such things as "likely to become a public charge," previous conviction of a crime, prostitution, and the like, as grounds for exclusion or deportation. Plainly, it was an aid to citizens, administrators, and the courts to combine this subject matter into one statute. This does not mean that it is invariably a good idea to consolidate—as the skeptic says, "It all depends."

I have mixed feelings about the advantages and disadvantages of codification. In some areas of the law there are unquestionably advantages due to greater certainty and uniformity, but in other areas codification is either not indicated or should be proceeded with cautiously. If in advance of codification responsibility could be squarely placed for updating the code, the risks would be greatly reduced. But U.S. experience to date is not reassuring on that score. Perhaps now that sunset laws (laws expunging outmoded statutes) are widely popular, U.S. lawmakers will develop those habits of mind that give greater assurance that codification could be made to work. It is, however, a job for the government rather than outside groups, and until government can be made more effective by dominant public opinion supporting it, the wisdom of a universal codification program being undertaken prematurely is questionable.

Freund's lifelong preoccupation with uniform state laws will now be examined. Freund had a passion for this movement, which occupied much of his time from 1908 until his death in 1932, for at least three good reasons. The first has been mentioned: there is altogether too much attention given to court decisions and not enough to legislation. Second, Freund looked upon uniform state laws as the most practicable way of countering the rapid (and to him, excessive) growth of federal centralization under the commerce and taxing powers.[2] Third, uniform state laws were another way of providing order and certainty into the law and hence making it more like the European model Freund admired. He became president of the National Conference of Commissioners on Uniform State Laws in 1920, and personally drafted model uniform laws in those areas in which he was most interested, namely, marriage, divorce, illegitimacy, guardianship, child labor, workmen's compensation, and working conditions.

The considerations that apply to the uniform state law movement are similar to those affecting the codification issue. The objective of providing a counterpoise to federal centralization is worth a considerable gamble. Second, the main motivation and achievement of the movement has been in the field of commercial law. Certainly there can be no question about the merits and social utility of this. If a country of continental size is to have a free flow of commerce, there must be a certain consistency about such things as credit, collections, and sanctions. Uniform state laws have been effective in this area, and hence this alone would be sufficient reason to support the movement. Third, although there always have been enthusiastic supporters of uniform state laws, the pace of reform has been slow and steady, and hence usually sound, rather than precipitate and spectacular. It has been nothing like the steamrollering that took place at the time of the Walter-Logan Bill of 1938, or the eventual passage of the Administrative Procedure Act of 1946 and its implementation following World War II.

The greatest danger in the movement is the one suggested by Brandeis's words "insulated laboratories." There is no question that one of the advantages of federalism is the frequency with which an innovation in one state rapidly becomes adopted in others, without running the risk of all states' experimenting with something that may not work. Communication has become so rapid that if Colorado announces the success of sunset laws today, Vermont (assuming the legislature is in session) may imitate it tomorrow. I would be willing to pay a high price for the freedom and innovativeness of this insulated laboratory system, as compared with that found in the Napoleanic tradition of centralization adopted by France and its neighbors. Centralization exists also in the USSR, but for different reasons. However, as has been observed, the farther you get from Moscow, the more freedom there is to diverge and innovate.

One final issue has a direct and weighty bearing on the life of the administrator. Should statutory law be long and detailed, in an effort to reduce the need for sublegislation by the administrator; or, on balance, is the modern practice of short, skeleton legislation more advantageous? There is currently a great need for more research in these areas. No one has really taken the place of Sir Courtenay Ilbert in Britain or Robert Luce in the United States as philosophers as well as technicians of the bill-drafting art. Nor is one likely to get this wisdom from any of the score or more of lawyers who do bill drafting for Congress on each side of the Capitol building. Such insights are more likely to come from an agency such as the Legislative Drafting Research Fund of Columbia University, which the late Joseph Chamberlain established with his own financial contributions.

The issue is essentially the same as the one Cooley and Dillon disagreed upon in the case of municipal corporations. Write detailed laws and you supposedly have more clarity, but you also run the risk of having the mandate strictly interpreted by the administrator as well as by the courts. Alternatively, write a shorter law and it allows more room for discretion, but since it is not detailed, it may be challenged in the courts more frequently than otherwise. I am not inclined to seize either horn of this dilemma. The ideal solution is to write a fairly short law, in plain English, but have it so well thought out both in terms of administrative utility and court approval that the law almost enforces itself.

In this case the law would be of moderate length and define discretionary areas as clearly as possible, but insofar as feasible would avoid mendicant words in favor of more operational ones. In other words, the idea in writing a statute is not to write an idealist's prayer but to stay as close as possible to the way an administrator thinks. Too many laws—some being ones I have worked on—sound too much like public relations' stunts. In contrast, my political belief is (possibly because I have the administrator's mind) that statutory legislation should encourage public expectations that can be realized, because to promise more than you can deliver is deficit politics.

It has been argued here that statutory law has as much claim to being legitimate law as the common law. If statutory law could be written more clearly and operationally, this fact alone would go far toward removing what lawyers call rule making (sublegislation) from the area of central controversy. Administrators should have an equal voice, with lawyers, in drafting legislation. Greater clarity sometimes can be produced by consolidating laws, codifying others, and making use of uniform state laws. The idea, however, is not to reduce everything to rule, but rather to provide guidelines within which discretion and innovation are possible. In short, the key to administrative law improvement is better draftsmanship. To assure this result, the administrator should initiate the law and its later amendments, while the legislature should carefully review, alter, and enact it.

As for the legislature as an institution, it is to be regreted that the American Bar Association has not concentrated its efforts on improving legislatures, instead of confining itself almost entirely to the administrative process as it has for over a generation. Congress has several functions, all important, such as appropriating funds, sharing responsibility for treaties and foreign policy, acting as a court of impeachment, educating the public, and testing and elevating public persons who gravitate into executive positions such as the presidency. But its two main functions are the making of law and sharing responsibility with the president for organizing, empowering, staffing, providing funds, and writing the substantive laws for the departments and agencies, which in terms of personnel and cost are 95 percent of the government. Legislatures need to be made more effective before administration can be improved. In times of crisis the legislature needs to learn to act with dispatch. The committee system needs to be simplified. More time should be spent on the managerial side of government, and this involves almost continual contact with the major action programs of the government.

The objective is greater accountability, while guaranteeing the necessary discretion. If contacts are frequent enough, this difficult balancing of factors can be made to succeed. My experience is that Congress usually trusts career executives when often it distrusts the more temporary political appointees whose average tenure in recent years has been something around two-and-a-half years. If Congress and the able career executive were to establish a closer partnership, government would begin to move with as much vigor as industry. Why not? They are both part of the same culture. But before this can happen business and the legal profession must want it to happen.

NOTES

1. Ernst Freund, *Standards of American Legislation* (Chicago: University of Chicago Press, 1917), p. 218.

2. Oscar Kraines, *The World and Ideas of Ernst Freund* (University, Ala.: University of Alabama Press, 1974), pp. 6, 60–65.

— *9* —

SUBLEGISLATION

The second major problem to be dealt with in Part II is what most legal writers now like to call rule making. Prior to the 1950s this concept was called sublegislation, which is a more descriptive and accurate term. It is by trying to reduce everything to rule that the legal profession has created so much red tape. Alternatively, if the emphasis is put on supplementing the work of legislature instead of on rules, the resulting focus on policy immediately energizes administration by loosening its shackles.

John P. Comer, who was one of the first writers to produce a book on this subject (and this as early as 1927), had the right idea when in *Legislative Functions of National Administrative Officers* (1927) he said that after any law, and especially a complicated one, has been passed, it has to be spelled out, the details filled in as a result of a step-by-step administrative procedure. Comer refers to this evolutionary process as "supplementary" or "detailed" legislation, made by administrators in pursuance of authority delegated to them by statutory provisions. Comer then suggested that there are two main kinds of supplementary legislation. The interpretive kind deals with the meaning of the statutory provisions. It is like saying, "In order that we may better understand each other, this is what it means to me." The second connotation goes further than the first: it adds to or supplements the law by making the provisions of the statute more concrete as authority flows through organization toward its ultimate objective, which is direct service to citizens. Comer points out that in the second, or operational phase, the administrator obviously needs a range of discretion. He is not merely interpreting; he is, in effect, adding to the law by making it more concrete and more operational.

One of the main shortcomings of jurists who try to reduce management to a hierarchy of rules is that they overlook the stimulus-response nature of law. Like everything in nature, law grows. It is spelled out when courts speak, and it is equally spelled out when the legislature or the administrative agency speaks. Law is not the monopoly of a profession or even of one branch of the government. It is something that grows and responds to society itself and all three branches take part in that response.

In his argument with the would-be rule maker, the administrator has the support of historians, sociologists, and practically the whole of the scientific community, all of whom believe in stimulus-response, evolutionary change, and adaptation. An example of this, by two jurists who were influenced by the theory of evolution, is Kocourek and Wigmore's Formative Influences in Legal Development (1918). In a chapter called "The Perpetual Evolution of Law," these authors point out that law is in an unceasing state of change. In its very essence it is shifting and protean. "Forever it is in the process of making and unmaking—a state of perpetual becoming." It is therefore an error to conclude that there is an absolutely fixed law either for epochs or for all time (pp. 667-68).

It is from sociology, however, more than from any other source, that clarification has come as to the division of labor in legal evolution. Philip Selznick, who heads an institute of legal research in California, illustrates this clear understanding of institutional teamwork in his book Law, Society, and Industrial Justice (1969), wherein he says that law is a great deal more than legal rules (p. 27). Law is generic and evolutionary and hence definitions should not be relied upon nearly so much as concepts (p. 4). The basic concept is that law is part and parcel of moral evolution, and hence part of the private-public nexus, the quest for a viable law of associations, and it is also an integral part of the political process (p. 28). And then this climax, which goes far toward legitimatizing the reason why administrators are inevitably involved in spelling out the law. Law, says Selznick, is part and parcel of the evolutionary attempt to clarify and fructify human ideals. The success of this evolutionary process depends in large part on "the enlargement of institutional competence to serve them" (that is, these evolutionary moral ideals) (p. 15). Consequently, if administration does not develop its own competence, the law will not grow and moral principles will not evolve. It is a team process.

Rules have very little to do with moral evolution and frequently, in excess, are a hindrance rather than an asset.

The strongest endorsement of the position being championed however, comes from a member of the legal profession who throughout the years has shown more insight into what administration is about than anyone in a law school position. Ralph Fuchs took the stand as early as 1939 that the attempted application of the judicial analogy to public administration is hackneyed, outmoded, and inept. Administration is not a loose assemblage of legislative and judicial characteristics—it has a unity and separate identity of its own. To use his own words, "the attempt to establish a significant classification of administrative functions on the basis of the separation of powers has definitely failed." Administrative functions are legislative functions, executive functions, quasi-legislative functions, or the like, but they are administrative functions. To fail to recognize the positive, dynamic character of administration (and administrative tribunals) is to miss the "very essence and reason for [their] existence."[1] No public administrator could put it more clearly or convincingly than that. Quasi-legislative authority is an incident to administrative work, not something separable from or foreign to it.

Over the years, it is possible that Emmette Redford of the University of Texas has contributed as much to an understanding of sublegislation as anyone else. In his book, *Administration of National Economic Control* (1952), this former Office of Price Administration official explains the rationale as follows: if the administrator is going to interpret statutory intent faithfully, he must make his standards known. As a result, "policy making and administration get mixed in the vast middle area of government hierarchy" (p. 67). This is, of course, the area of line or program management. Standards serve a triple purpose: they enable the agency to clarify specifically the policy it intends to follow; second, standards assure the even-handed treatment of all persons subject to the statute in question (this involves both substantive and procedural right); and third, it gives the executive the working tools for passing down the line to the field the true intent of the law and the standards of interpretation that need to be applied (p. 66).

There are two things about this statement that should be underscored. Note how Redford connects sublegislation with the flow of work. This is something the lawyers fail to do, with resulting distortion. Second, note also how Redford in his second point interprets fairness as both substantive and procedural due process. Again, the lawyers distort the complete picture because they regard administration almost exclusively as procedure.

There is a third respect in which Redford's treatment of this subject is perceptive and realistic. He shows the connection between what lawyers call "rule making" and "orders," or what is more simply called sublegislation and quasi-judicial decisions. The connective tissue is this: interpretation starts with the standard, proceeds through the directing (executive leadership) phase of administration, and frequently in the course of it particular (individual) decisions need to be made, in which case the same standards that apply to policy are germane to decision as well (p. 85). In other words, Redford recognizes the unity of the administrative process and the necessity of keeping it that way. The lawyer mind, in contrast, tries to divide it into three parts, like Gaul: rule making, orders, and the nondiscretionary work of clerks and paper-pushers. It is this attempt to emasculate the flow of work that makes the administrator so angry.

The administrator has no objection to the requirement that his sublegislation (policy, standards) and his orders (more important decisions) be published in the *Federal Register*. As long as this is done sensibly and without obvious intent to hamstring administrative enforcement, he favors the informational activity because it makes his overall task easier. (People favor things they understand; react instinctively against anything strange.) He does object, and rightly, to the unconscionable and absurd amount of time that hearings take before, under the terms of the Administrative Procedure Act, subleg-islation may even be promulgated in the *Federal Register*.

It is a matter of balance, of common sense. When these hearings are prolonged, as they often are when the pressure group is strong enough, the administrator realizes that one of two explanations predominates: either the lawyers are trying to feather their nests, or the regulated interests are trying to sabotage the intent of the law by excessive administrative delays. Where the amount of money is large enough, it is commonly both. Cynically enough, the attempted justification for this delaying tactic is "personal right," or "personal freedom." All too often it is either sabotage or greed.

The administrator has the same objection to the latest step in the legal profession's incursions. This take the form that administrative interpretation of the intent and standards to be applied must be approved by the legislature before they can be put into effect. This is done either by providing that the rules must lie before the legislature for a certain period of time, and if there is no objection they are then allowed to go into effect, or second, they must be expressly approved by a committee or committees of the legislature, sometimes a joint committee that is set up expressly for that purpose. This is the ultimate in humiliation. It says to the administrator, "We can trust professionals in the judicial branch but not professionals in the administrative branch." They are reduced, in effect, to second-class citizens, and their resentment is like that of any minority that is treated like second-class citizens. And all this because as a result of constant propaganda the administrative professional is stigmatized as a bureaucrat, suggesting an incompetent, a eunuch. No other country treats its professionals so shamefully. These same men and women are often scientists, or others who have been attracted away from corporations and universities because of their altruistic desire to work for the entire public. To treat them this way deserves the use of the word "shameful."

Taken over the entire period since *Field* v. *Clark* (143 U.S. 649, 12 S.Ct. 495) (1892), the Supreme Court of the United States cannot be blamed for the unreasonable restrictions on administrative authority relative to delegation. On the contrary, its record is only to be applauded, because the Court always has shown a better grasp of what is entailed in administration than the organized bar has exhibited since 1946, when the Administrative Procedure Act was put into effect. An example of this is found in Mr. Justice Frankfurter's opinion in *FCC* v. *RCA Communications, Inc.* (346 U.S. 86, 73 S.Ct. 998), in 1953, when he observed that,

> The statutory standard no doubt leaves wide discretion and calls for imaginative interpretation. Not a standard that lends itself to application with exactitude, it expresses a policy, born of years of unhappy trial and error, that is "as concrete as the complicated factors for judgment in such a field of delegated authority permit."

It is the Court's responsibility, he continued, "to say whether the Commission has been guided by proper considerations in bringing the deposit of its experience, the disciplined feel of the expert, to bear on applications for licenses in the public interest. . . ."

In 1940, while the Attorney-General's Committee on Administrative Procedure was still at work, the Supreme Court in *Sunshine Anthracite Coal Company* v. *Adkins*, (310 U.S. 381, 60 S.Ct. 907) stated the real reason why delegation has always been looked upon as a practical necessity, saying, "Delegation by Congress has long been recognized as necessary *in order that the exertion of legislative power does not become a futility*." Only in two cases, says Kenneth Davis, have congressional delegations to public authorities been held invalid. Both were justifiably famous cases, the *Panama Refining* (1935) and the *Schechter Poultry* (1935) cases. Davis defends this seeming retreat by the Supreme Court from a consistent, statesmanlike position on grounds that were so exceptional as to be justified. First, neither delegation was to a regularly constituted agency that followed established procedures for assuring customary safeguards to affected parties. Second, the *Panama* decision, says Davis, was influenced by "exceptional executive disorganization," and in the absence of such a situation would not be followed today. Third, the *Schechter* decision, in the National Recovery Administration controversy, entailed an excessive delegation of the kind that Congress is not likely to make again (*Administrative Law and Government*, 1960, p. 55). Of course, these are matters of opinion in trying to explain what happened, and they overlook the climate of the time; in general, however, there can be no doubt about the soundness of Davis's conclusions.

Davis, like many lawyers, justifies rule making on the ground that it is democratic, "a miniature democratic process . . . at work." Of course, it is this, but it can become excessive. He cites an instance, for example, where in deciding on conditions for transporting household goods, the Interstate Commerce Commission, in a single rulemaking procedure, conducted 89 informal conferences throughout the country, attended by 1,740 individuals representing 1,286 motor carriers (*Administrative Law and Government* p. 69). Davis does not say how much time this took or how much knowledge it added. He does say that the ICC, in questionnaires, asked, "Do you want this?" or "What do you want?" What this overlooks is that the agency could have used the questionnaire in any case, and, second, that administrative agencies see their clientele every working day and hence know far more about what they want and what their input is than lawyers give them credit for. Often the main purpose is to educate the lawyers, not the administrators.

My experience in labor, immigration, and shipping was that hardly a day, and certainly not more than a week, went by without having a scheduled appointment with most major and minor interests and their legislative lobbyists. If the administrator is fair-minded, and not biased, both sides flow through his office doors more freely than they would into a formal hearing or a court of law. In recruiting executive personnel, therefore, high rating should be given to persons who have judicial temperaments. It saves much time and money and frequently produces superior results.

I am inclined to think that there is really only one form that sublegislation takes. The declaratory subcategory is unnecessary. Whenever a new agency is set up or a new statute is added to its jurisdiction, the first thing it does is interpret the statute in the process of setting goals and policies. These are the very same standards that are followed in Comer's second classification, the supplementary or what I call the instrumental category. In other words, all attempts to breathe life and create tissue in the law are basically instrumental. They are the connective tissue between aspiration and accomplishment. I do not think it necessary that everyone think this way. But for my part, as an administrator I find this solution more comfortable than the dual classification, which is only an unwarranted invitation to lawyers to interfere.

If there is so much unanimity between the Supreme Court and the early ideas of lawyers like Frankfurter and public administrators like Redford, why has rule making become so obsessive that for some it is a crusade, and for others a plague?

The answer is to be found in the period between 1938, when the Supreme Court was declaring New Deal legislation unconstitutional, and 1944 when, with World War II almost over, the American Bar Association moved to put teeth into administrative procedure legislation, after the Walter-Logan Act of 1938 had been vetoed by Roosevelt.

In brief, the chronology is as follows:

1933: This was the first year of the New Deal. The American Bar Association created a special committee on administrative law, which in 1934 commenced a series of annual reports. The battle cry was "The judicial branch of the federal government is being undermined."

1938: Roscoe Pound, who then headed the committee, reported ten tendencies of administrative agencies that were threatening— such as to decide without a hearing, to hear only one side, to consider evidence not produced, and to fail to allow attorneys to appear in many kinds of hearing. The Walter-Logan bill was passed but vetoed. In a strongly worded statement, President Roosevelt charged conservative bias against the New Deal and a thinly veiled conspiracy of lawyers to make more work and power for themselves. (Roosevelt, himself, had been trained as a lawyer.)

1939: Influenced by his attorney-general, in February Roosevelt authorized the appointment of a committee to investigate "the need for procedural reform in the field of administrative law." It was a well done research job and produced a monograph on many action programs, including immigration. Many lawyers, like Davis and Fuchs, received an invaluable education concerning administration as a result of their field work.

1941: *The Final Report*, consisting of 474 pages, appeared. The main subjects dealt with were rule making and administrative adjudication. Eleven chapters dealt with the administrative process, administrative information, informal methods of adjudication, formal adjudication, judicial review of administrative adjudication, procedure in administrative rule making, Office of Federal Administrative Procedure (new), and recommendations concerning individual agencies. Its statement of objectives was seemingly above reproach: equally to promote the public interest and the effective administration of the law, while at the same time guaranteeing impartial justice to all private interests ("Introduction," p. 2).

The main focus, like that of the legal profession, was upon the independent regulatory tribunals, the majority of which, like the Securities and Exchange Commission, the Federal Communications Commission, and the National Labor Relations Board, had been created during the New Deal period.

If the reform had stopped with a report, many of the problems dealt with in this book would not, perhaps, have arisen. But once the recommendations were legislatively institutionalized and a separate agency was set up within the administration to judicialize both rule and order making, a foothold was secured from which the power and influence of lawyers has been steadily advanced so that today the only way of removing the excesses would be to abolish the procedural agencies and start all over again. This period, as said earlier, did not start until 1944, because it was only after World War II was mostly over that the American Bar Association renewed its insistence that the legislation be passed and the act be made operational. This in itself is instructive, because it is doubtful that World War II could have been conducted as successfully as it was if all the provisions of the 1946 legislation had been in effect during the war.

There is no doubt, as Davis says, that the AP Act was a great triumph for the American Bar Association, undoubtedly the greatest achievement in its history. The avowed objectives it sought were to bring back the decision of controversies of all kinds to the judicial system; to assure that life tenure shall be guaranteed to all who exercise judicial functions; and to eliminate the threat of "administrative absolutism," which they equated with Marxism. (*Administrative Law and Government*, p. 29) However, as Davis notes, it did not actually pull back the judicial cases from administrative agencies and guarantee the courts a monopoly. Instead, it put the courts into administration, in their primary jurisdiction, thus weakening both sublegislation and quasi-adjudication by shattering the unity of the administrative process.

I would not go so far as James Landis did when referring to the Walter-Logan bill: "cut off a foot here and there a head, leaving broken and bleeding the processes of administrative law."[2] Instead, I would compare it to the "ruleitis" that every administrator is tempted to promote at one time or another, and that subtly but irresistibly saps the life of dynamic administration as it bureaucratizes it in the derogatory sense.

The way that the Attorney-General's Committee rationalized its conclusions concerning rule making is extremely interesting (*Final Report*, pp. 101–02). First, they say that administrative agencies are not like legislatures: the latter deal with a cross-section of the community and hence are like a jack-of-all-trades. The administrative agency, in contrast, has a narrower constituency, operates in the open, needs a great deal of discretion, and has more time than a legislature for perfecting its sublegislation. (Nothing at all is said about the execution of the law, which of course is its main business.)

Since the administrative agency, they argue, presumably has lots of time, it should follow four steps in rule making: investigation or study of the problems to be dealt with; formulation of tentative ideas regarding the regulations (standards, policies) to be issued; the testing of these ideas; and the final formulation of the regulations (*Final Report*, p. 102).

This shows no real understanding of what administration is all about. Administration is not playing games, reporting on a case in a law school class, or figuring out the probabilities in the theory of games. Administration is work. Production. Accomplishment. The administrator does not need to go through this rigmarole. He does research continuously. It is not an intensive investigation of individual controversies, as in a courtroom. Administration deals with systems, and systems cannot be maintained without constant research. That is what experts are for.

As for the other three points made by the committee, any experienced administrator knows that tentative policy positions, followed by prolonged hearings and delay before a mature policy position may be promulgated, is senseless and unworkable. There should be only one hearing, with careful preparation in advance. Interested parties should have a chance to study the policy or standard in advance. Then, after consideration, if any modification of the original policy or standard is thought desirable by the administrator (who initially has the authority and the discretion), the modified statement may be circulated to interested parties, but without the necessity of another formal hearing.

If business were required to operate the way the public administrator is expected to conduct himself, the enterprise system would collapse.

In making these critical comments I do not wish to be interpreted as being generally critical of the research that went into the *Final*

Report of the Attorney-General's Committee on Administrative Procedure. It was an excellent research job. Politically, I think Roosevelt and his attorney-general made a great mistake in trying to mollify the American Bar Association at the time they did. There may be a number of possible explanations for this. The president lost his "cool" in denouncing lawyers and their associations and probably regretted his burst of temper afterward. He probably figured that the conservative attack to this point had been centered on his legislation—the substantive aspect—and hence decided that it would do no great harm to have a study made of procedure, because that sounded innocuous enough.* His mistake consisted in two false assumptions: he failed to see that once the conservatives got a foothold in the government they could use it to hamstring administration whenever it suited their interest to do so; and second, Roosevelt should have known, and doubtless did in hindsight, that those who talk human rights, when what they mean is business interests, cannot be expected to reform, no matter what attempt at reconciliation is offered them.

In hindsight also, it seems clear that if the report had been confined to the independent regulatory commissions and what to do with them, that would have been infinitely better than imposing shackles on the entire administrative side of government. Also, it would have been easier to modify or remove the procedural restraints afterward. Politically, it is a difficult feat to relax the restraints once they have been imposed. There is no organized lobby for the public interest as there is for lawyers and their conservative clients. People are duped by talk of private rights and do not see the economic cunning lying beneath. It is possible, therefore, that the situation may continue largely unchanged until, at some time when the country tries to figure out why its position in the world is declining, a hard look is taken at government; then it may be decided that administration ought to be freer if it is to become effective. It will be a real test for representative government.

Among the first scholarly experts to recognize the danger to administrative effectiveness inherent in the Administrative Procedure Act were a husband-and-wife team, Frederick Blachly and Miriam Oatman. They were employed by the Brookings Institution, had already published *Federal Regulatory Action and Control* (1940), and were rather mild-mannered individuals. In 1946, however, when the law was finally passed, they wrote "The Sabotage of the Administra-

---

* Having been in Justice at the time and close to the administration, this is the way I remember it.

tive Process" (*Public Administration Review*, vol. 6). This article is well worth reading because it not only accurately foretells the impediments that the act imposes upon dynamic administration, but it also criticizes the procedures followed by the committees in considering the bills.

Another careful and knowledgeable scholar, Ferrell Heady of the University of Michigan, wrote a book called *Administrative Procedure Legislation in the States* (1952), and got to the heart of the difficulty in these words:

> Statutes can set minimum standards which must be observed, making a contribution in a *negative* way to the betterment of regulatory procedure. But legislation cannot provide a *positive* incentive for *continuous improvement* in procedure. This must come from agency *initiative*, aided by advice and encouragement from the outside. The legislature is in a position to correct deficiencies which come to its attention, but it cannot by a statutory provision ensure a high caliber of *competence* in regulatory agencies or instill a *sense of responsibility* . . . in the minds of administrative officials for perfecting fair and balanced procedure (p. 120) [emphasis added].

Heady then enunciates this principle: "general statutes setting procedure may be less effective and potentially more dangerous . . . than are procedural provisions which appear in the *individual* statutes governing the powers and goals of the various regulatory agencies (p. 120) [emphasis added]. Therefore his general conclusion was, "General procedural legislation must assume a burden of proof that it is supplying procedural guides which the separate regulatory statutes have for some reason failed to provide, and that these guides do not amount to procedural straitjackets hampering the legitimate movements of the regulatory agencies" (p. 121). Heady also concluded that "there is a point of diminishing returns in imposing formalized and uniform procedural requirements." This point, he says, "has been reached and passed by pending procedural reforms which enjoy potent support and are receiving serious support in some of the states covered" in his study (p. 122). This was written in 1952 and since then the situation has become much worse, as he and others predicted it would.

To the same effect was a conclusion reached by Robert M. Benjamin, in his comprehensive *Administrative Adjudication in New York State* (1942). A general procedural code in the interest of uniformity is neither feasible nor desirable. Diversity exists for reasons that are not merely valid but inescapable. Even if uniformity were thought desirable, the task of drafting a procedural code creates great, if not insuperable, difficulties of terminology. Finally, says Benjamin, if all other problems could be surmounted, the results would soon become "illusory" (pp. 35–36).

In his book *An Introduction to Administrative Law* (1950), James Hart of the University of Virginia included in his "Introduction" an excellent summary of the administrative assumptions of the so-called Acheson Committee that framed the *Final Report* of the Attorney-General's Committee on Administrative Procedure of 1940. This is found in a chapter of the *Final Report* called "The Origins, Development, and Characteristics of the Administrative Process," which is a preface to *Administrative Procedures in Government Agencies*. Herein are found the two reasons why the Committee went wrong.

The first error, in my view, was this: the "distinguishing feature" of an administrative agency, said the Committee, is "the power to determine, either by rule or by decision, *private rights and obligations*." This is one objective, but clearly not the main one. The main one is to give effect to the legislative mandate in all its dimensions.

The second error was that the Committee had a limited view of what administration entails. As Hart points out, the Attorney-General's Committee discussed some of the difficulties that Blachly-Oatman, Heady, Benjamin, and others point out, but ultimately they adopted a distorted view of how administration needs to operate. They paid lip service to the idea that administrative agencies frequently have large staffs, many duties, that they need to reconcile efficiency and fairness, and that they need to utilize to the fullest degree the special skills and expertise at the agency's command. Then they said that as part of the process of delegation there needs to be a division of labor. The basic division is between the executives and the staff. Next they posed the assumption that the executives cannot afford to lose their sense of direction in a host of details (Hart, "Introduction," p. 8).

This is where they went wrong. The Committee's idea was that administration is Olympian. A few individuals sit on the heights and enjoy splendid isolation from those people who do routine work, the rank and file who are beneath them in the hierarchy. From this the Committee concluded that if a general statute, such as theirs, were to lay down uniform rules of procedure, the routine rank-and-file people would be enabled to do their work largely without direction or leadership. This, in turn, would give the executives more leisure to think and guarantee that they did not lose their sense of direction. In other words, executives, like a court, wait until someone brings a case or a decision to them for action.

Such assumptions are a caricature or a charade, probably both. This is not the way administration operates nor can it be expected to produce results. Splintering destroys unity, leadership, the meshing of line and staff, and with this produces neutralized administration. Executives are people who have more facts than anyone else, who follow every phase of work closely, and whose "distinguishing feature" (to use the Committee's phrase) is to integrate everything the agency does—the substantive as well as the procedural, the policy as well as the organizational flow, the spelling out of legislative intent as well as the decisions that are made every day, the control and the evaluation of results.

It is the old problem of logic. Start with wrong assumptions and you get wrong results.

In 1971 when a task force I headed for the President's Advisory Council on Executive Organization (the Ash Council) brought out a report called *A New Regulatory Framework*, the consequences of the Acheson style of thinking that entered into the 1940 *Final Report* could be seen clearly by the conservative Republican committee members who signed the report:

> Deficiences in the performance of the regulatory commissions are partly due to the difficulty of attracting highly qualified commissioners and retaining executive staff. Even able administrators have difficulty in serving as coequals on collegial commissions.
>
> While there are notable exceptions, it is difficult to attract to regulatory positions men of skill in administration and breadth of perspective largely because of the procedures and traditions associated with appointment to regulatory commissions (p. 4).

The overemphasis on procedure and overjudicialization, concluded the report, "precludes coordination of agency policy and priorities with those of the executive branch" (p. 5).

When conservative business executives begin to think about management as business managers commonly do, and hence insist that the government be run on sound administrative lines, the excesses of the 1946 legislation will be radically offset in favor of something that will work.

In the light of what has transpired, Hart's observations concerning the intent of the Acheson committee are ironic. In 1941, says Hart, the finding was that there were nine executive departments and 18 independent agencies that should become the main focus of the attorney-general's solicitude. Later, however, by taking "the largest possible units," the Committee decided that "a more accurate picture was presented by the statement that fifty-one agencies exercised administrative powers" ("Introduction," p. 3). "Administrative" powers? This, in itself, reveals that the committee was using one word to describe something that bears no relation to reality! What has happened since then, of course, is that the entire executive branch suffers from the effect of the Committee's original assumptions. Moreover, there is now an unholy alliance between the legalists and the public personnel profession.

Many academic administrative lawyers have kept their balance despite the "triumphs" ushered in by the administrative procedure acts of Congress and several states. Others, like Bernard Schwartz, are still celebrating the lawyers' victory. The *Morgan* cases of 1938–41, says this authority, shifted the emphasis to administrative procedure. After 35 years of working out the pattern in regulatory tribunals, says Schwartz, the procedural emphasis has been extended to "the newer areas of social welfare" with federal and state procedure acts. This was the turning point, the new day (*Administrative Law*, 1977, p. 22).

Schwartz then goes on to observe that there is current disillusionment with the administrative process; too often it has proved more time-consuming and costly than the judicial process; there has been an increasing failure of welfare agencies to protect the very public interest they were created to serve; administration has become "an established part of the economic status quo." As examples of social welfare, Schwartz lists such things as Social Security, disability, welfare, aid to dependent children, health care, and a growing list of other services that have come under the guardianship [sic] of the administrative process. Then his exultant climax: "The law has pressed these newer areas into the judicialized mold of the regulatory process" (p. 23). Schwartz has no confidence in administration and hence expects it to fail without the overlordship of the legal profession.

One comes full circle, therefore, to the theme enunciated in the preceding chapter on drafting the statutory law. What is needed is better legislation, with the administrative branch assured enough independence to make its efforts unified and effective. Sublegislation is an integral part of administration and is not a conquered province presided over by lawyers and their contentious proceedings. Rule making, says Lloyd D. Musolf in his monograph *Federal Examiners and the Conflict of Law and Administration* (1952), is logically carried out by means of an informational hearing, with varying degrees of informality. Almost immediately after 1946, however, due to the pressure of bar associations on Congress, it has become increasingly formalized. This takes the form of statutory directives requiring that when a rule is promulgated, it be based on the record of testimony complied at the hearing (pp. 59–60). Even when the law has flatly exempted certain types of proceedings in which rule making is involved, some agencies, notably the Interstate Commerce Commission and the Federal Power Commission, immediately began "to cast their legislative functions in a judicial mould." This, as Musolf points out, was done despite the fact that diversity of treatment was recognized by the Attorney-General's Committee as being necessary to keeping the administrative process resilient and flexible (pp. 85–86).

Hence the irony. The Administrative Procedure Act was designed to stop the creeping paralysis of bureaucracy. Now that it has been passed, the problem is to stop the creeping paralysis of judicialization from subverting the Republic.

NOTES

1. Ralph Fuchs, "Symposium on Administrative Law," *American Law School Review* 60 (1939): 142; idem, "Concepts and Policies in Anglo-American Administrative Law Theory," *Yale Law Journal* 47 (February 1938): 538–76.

2. James Landis, "Crucial Issues in Administration Law," *Harvard Law Review* 53 (1940): 1,077, 1,102.

— 10 —

JUDICIALIZING ADMINISTRATION

Not only have the lawyers invaded and weakened the program administrator's responsibility for policy, but they also have turned the internal work program of administration into something resembling a courtroom procedure, a procedure carried on by judges who are appointed by an outside agency. Hence for both reasons, sublegislation and administrative adjudication, the trend of the past 30 years may be called "the judicializing of administration," and it is against this that this book protests. If government is to surmount its problems, management needs to be strong and authentic.

Those who write textbooks on public administration have used the expression administrative adjudication for a long time, and were quite comfortable with it. But this was before the Administrative Procedure Act was passed. To their way of thinking, certain decisions resembled what courts do, and so they used the term administrative adjudication. Decision making and administrative adjudication were differentiated quite clearly. Whole books were written on the decision-making process as it applies to everything the administrator does: setting objectives, deciding on public policy, organization, personnel management, and public relations. Administrative decision making, in contrast, meant deciding cases that courts might have decided or that the legislature had entrusted to an administrative agency in order to relieve the load of the judiciary.

After the Administrative Procedure Act was passed, administrative adjudication came to mean something else. It became a lawyer's term, not an administrator's. Adjudication was carved out of administration instead of being an integral part of it; the atmosphere of the courtroom was substituted for the institutional decision of the agency; those who were called administrative judges were on a separate payroll; the administrator felt left out; his unified jurisdiction was weakened in a vital area and his drive and self-confidence were diminished.

Before the Administrative Procedure Act came into existence, decisions were made by the regular administrative staff, with the ultimate decision being entrusted to the head of the agency. Characteristically, it was a collective or institutional decision, each making his contribution and all checking each other. The decisions were made on the basis of statutory law, plus agency sublegislation, plus decided court cases. The system worked, and in most cases worked well. Then the idea arose of using "hearing examiners" in certain cases where hearings were long and technical, as in railroad cases coming under the Interstate Commerce Commission. This represented no breach of principle: administration was still integrated and coordinated.

When the Administrative Procedure Act of 1946 was enacted, however, judicialization was speeded up, and now, like a spreading fog, it has become well-nigh universal. It began with hearing officers who were recruited by the U.S. Civil Service Commission and put in a pool, from which they were assigned to various agencies. At first these hearing officers were used only in specified agencies, but from time to time the number of agencies was added to as a result of lawyer pressure. Then the idea of courtroom procedure was still further enlarged when Congress created the office of "Administrative Judge," this being one who operates inside the agency instead of outside it, as in the case of European administrative courts.

Theoretically, the recommended decision of the administrative judge is not final. The responsible executive of the agency in question makes the decision. He can accept the decision, overrule the recommended decision, or send the case back for further proceedings.

This is the theory. In actual practice, however, the longer the system has been in existence, the more frequently the recommended decision becomes the final decision. There are a number of reasons for this: the chief executive is busy with other things; under the new system he is not required to follow the development of the case; he finds it difficult to check on the decision because formerly he could rely upon his entire organization and now this area has been carved out and given to someone else; if the executive thinks the proposed decision is wrong, it is almost as if the burden of proof were on the executive to prove the judge in error; and finally, so great is the average U.S. citizen's deference to the term "judge," that the operating executive hesitates to question anyone with such a designation.

It is a clever way of setting up an empire within an empire. The hearing officers and administrative judges are on a different payroll. Moreover, unlike other officials in his department or agency, the executive is expressly forbidden to fire, discipline, or even communicate with the administrative judge except under very special circumstances, which usually means when the judge submits his proposed order. Under the old system, the entire resources of the agency could be relied upon in making an institutional decision. Under the new system, the judge is isolated in the same manner as a judicial judge, for fear that improper influence will be brought to bear upon him.

The atmosphere of administration, which ought to be positive and dynamic, therefore has become increasingly contentious and neutralizing. Even the term that is used to describe a decision—the word "order"—conveys this idea of domination and the authoritarian personality, instead of the practitioner of human relations who excels at getting people to cooperate.

What is an order? A look at the Act itself would be informative. Here one learns that adjudication means agency process for the formulation of an order. An order is defined in these words: "The whole or part of a final disposition, whether affirmative, negative, injunctive, or declaratory in form, of an agency in a matter other than rule making but including licensing."

Simple, isn't it? If I were an administrator under today's conditions, I would know that an order is what my legal adviser tells me it is because I would unquestionably be under his orders.

The worst part of this whole business is that the Act, with amendments, did not stop at requiring actual adjudication in the case of only certain kinds of agencies such as the Federal Communications Commission. In any case it would have to have held formal hearings at the time licenses were awarded, renewed, or revoked. Instead, it applied the adjudication requirement to the whole of government. Paragraph 553 of the 1946 Act dealing with adjudication starts out, "This section applies . . . in every case of adjudication required by statute," and then proceeds to list the exceptions, such as the conduct of military or foreign affairs. In other words, although in other respects the Administrative Procedure Act used the foot-in-the-door technique and then extended its influence by steady accretion, when it came to converting decisions into adjudications, the sponsors felt strong enough, initially, to judicialize openly the conduct of administrative affairs.

Nor was this all. The legislation then proceeded to set up hearing examiners, who had been used sparingly in a few instances prior to this time and were now to become a universal fixture,[1] tying them into the United States Civil Service Commission and an independent board. Then, later, these judges who operated inside administration, were to be given the title of administrative judges. To top this off, in Chapter 7 the legislation sets forth in detail what needs to be done to get a judicial review of administrative adjudications. Then to make sure that there was no fudging in the judicialization of administration that had been won, Congress set up in 1961 the Administrative Conference of the United States to study the possible improvement of administrative procedures, continuing the false assumption that administration is merely procedure in the lawyer's sense of that abused term.

I am satisfied that we need a new start. The sweeping judicialization requirement should be repealed, and if there is need for guidelines, they should be incorporated into the legislation empowering the individual agency. Second, hearing officers should not constitute a pool from which they circulate throughout the government; again, if hearing officers are needed they should be provided for, agency by agency. Third, administrative judges are needed, but they should be outside of administration as in any proper court system, not inside it. The unholy link with the Civil Service Commission and its personnel legalists should be broken. So likewise should the Administrative Conference of the United States be abolished, and something like a National Management Foundation (modelled after the National Science Foundation) should take its place. In an act of great generosity, lawyers should not be absolutely barred from membership in the Foundation!

Musolf points to the heart of the difficulty in these words: "Like courts, administrative agencies employ the adjudicatory process; unlike courts they employ it only incidentally to their broad end of implementing a statute" (*Federal Examiners and the Conflict of Law and Administration,* pp. 12–13). Or, putting the problem in its larger, semantic setting: decision is the universal category; administrators, like courts, make decisions; some of the decisions made by administrative agencies may be as important as some judicial decisions, but for the government as a whole they are clearly less than 1 percent of the total. When, therefore, 1 percent is treated as if it were 90 percent or more, the tail wags the dog.

The best treatment of this subject in philosophical depth is by Emmette Redford of the University of Texas in an article called "Regulation Revisted."[2] With his usual prescience, Redford enunciates a number of related propositions, as follows:

Administration is the most diverse of the categories of government action.

Administration is movement from task delegation to system structure, and then to system maintenance.

Administration is nevertheless one of the sources for policy initiative in the American system.

Attributes of administrative behavior are more pervasive than administrative form (structure). Structure may nevertheless be significant.

Needs to be satisfied in administrative operations are numerous.

And finally, the main problem in representative government is not rules or adjudication, but political responsibility.

He then points out that the needs to be satisfied in administrative operations are six in number: policy planning, policy coordination, policy leadership, policy responsibility, policy and program evaluation, and correlation of internal tasks (p. 553).

It must have been a fortunate confluence of zodiacal influences that gave the American Bar Association the Supreme Court's decision in the first *Morgan* case in 1936 (298 U.S. 468, 56 S.Ct. 906). This, combined with other decisions holding some of the main pieces of New Deal legislation unconstitutional, provided just the milieu that was needed to throttle the government. The Department of Agriculture had become one of the largest in the government. Like the Department of Labor, it was a seedbed of new legislation. The secretaries of Agriculture, Labor, and Commerce served as a threesome on Roosevelt's subcommittee of his Cabinet called the Committee on Economic Security. The *Morgan* case involved the right of the Secretary of Agriculture to regulate stockyard transactions in Kansas City. The issue was whether he had to do it personally or could delegate the task. The Supreme Court held that he who decides must hear. This was good judicial doctrine but poor administrative doctrine. Then they held, and this gave the impetus to judicialization of the entire administrative process that was needed, that:

It is a proceeding looking to legislative action in the fixing of rates in market agencies. And, while the order [note the double use of this term] is legislative . . . it is a proceeding which by virtue of the authority conferred has special attributes—Congress has required the Secretary to . . . "determine and prescribe" what shall be the just and reasonable rate. . . . It is a duty which carries with it fundamental *procedural* requirements. *There must be a full hearing.* There must be evidence adequate to support pertinent and necessary

> findings of fact. . . . A proceeding of this sort requiring the taking
> and weighing of evidence, and the making of an order supported by
> such finds, *has a quality resembling that of a judicial proceeding*.

Hence, continued the court, it is frequently described as a proceeding of a quasi-judicial character. The requirement of a "full hearing" has obvious reference to the tradition of judicial proceedings.

I can recall vividly how this dictum reverberated throughout Washington and caused wide consternation among administrators. In effect, it threatened to abolish the institutional decision, which may be described as one made by an administrative agency and not exclusively by an official or by agency heads.[3] It said, in effect, that if the Secretary of Agriculture did not personally decide, no one else would be allowed to decide. Under these circumstances the Department of Agriculture, in much of its work, would have been brought to a virtual standstill.

The first *Morgan* case was not only bad law, but it also was arrived at by tortuous reasoning, in which quasi legislation and quasi-judicial action were completely scrambled. It illustrates, as clearly as any case in the long history of the Supreme Court ever did, the dangers inherent in reasoning from a dubious analogy. On top of this, it flew directly in the face of the 1908 decision in *Prentis* v. *Atlantic Coast Line* (211 U.S. 210, 226; 29 S.Ct. 67, 69), in which the court held, in a decision rendered by Mr. Justice Holmes, that

> A judicial inquiry investigates, declares, and enforces liabilities as
> they stand on present or past facts and under laws supposed
> already to exist. This is its purpose and end. Legislation, on the
> other hand, looks to the future and changes conditions by making a
> new rule, to be applied thereafter to all or some part of those subject
> to its power. The establishment of a rate is the making of a rule for
> the future, and therefore is an act legislative, not judicial in kind. . . .

One may question whether the making of a rate is, in fact, a quasi-legislative act. I would argue that it is neither legislative nor judicial, but administrative. But the important point to lay hold of at the moment is that since 1908, rate making had not been considered a judicial act, even by analogy.

The second *Morgan* case seemed to contradict some of the implications left by the first decision.[4] Finally, in the third *Morgan* case, *United States* v. *Morgan* (312 U.S. 409, 61 S.Ct. 999), Mr. Justice Frankfurter, speaking for the Court, noted that this case had been to the Supreme Court periodically over a period of 11 years. He called attention to the obvious difficulties of any court's attempting "to probe the mental processes of the Secretary" of Agriculture; said it was not an appropriate activity for a court to undertake, and suggested the dubious nature of trying to examine the circulation of memoranda internally within the Department of Agriculture in an attempt to judge whether the secretary had been fully and fairly apprised of what was taking place.

So it was a partial victory for the beleaguered administrator. Not so entirely, however, because by this time the Court's focus had turned to the question of whether hearing examiners had been given sufficient recognition and power within the internal operations of administration, in lieu of judicial judges. This laid the foundation for another big advance in the ultimate judicialization of the administrative process, a development that has skewed managerial performance ever since. Lloyd Musolf notes this triumph clearly in these words: "If administrative procedure, not judicial review of administrative action, was the key to controlling regulatory administration, then it seemed *logical to suppose that the examiner was even closer to the core of the administrative process than the agency heads, who reviewed his work* (Federal Examiners and the Conflict of Law and Administration, p. 41).

In the end, therefore, the American Bar Association won its battle. If administration was not to be fully judicialized from the outside, it might be even more effectively judicialized from the inside.

A neglected area of judicialization is the psychological aspect. Except for program managers who may have strong personalities and who see the deadening effect of excessive rules, formalities, and Gilbert-and-Sullivan procedures, the rest of the government has a fatal fascination with judicial paraphernalia. This is to be expected in legislatures where lawyers are so numerous and where frequently the Judiciary Committee has a power and influence unequaled by any other committee (they and the appropriations committee frequently team up to thwart progressive legislation).

Inside the bureaucracy, the appeal of ruleitis is almost entirely psychological. The government is large and impersonal and individuals feel dwarfed and threatened by it.[5] They attempt to offset the splintering effect of size and impersonality by creating enclaves of certainty with which they identify. Legalization and judicialization are perfect instruments for meeting this neurotic need. It gives administrators a feeling of security to make rules for themselves and provides the facsimile of power when they impose rules on others. The more they fall into the habit of routine procedure the less they have to think. When someone comes along and says, "let us judicialize the administrative process," therefore, the prospect is immediately appealing except for those who have strong altruistic or patriotic motivations. "Sure," say the others, "let the judge do it—then he, not I, will have the responsibility."

The administrator knows he has to fight this tendency constantly. Many lawyers, being shortsighted, like to exploit it. The administrator is a fighter. The lawyer, unless principled like his administrator counterpart, is often the superb manipulator.

One of the ways of overcoming this difficulty is for lawyers as well as administrators to probe more deeply than most have done into the decision process. This is a relatively new field for intensive cultivation in the United States and may become significant because it represents an interdisciplinary, behaviorist approach to what is involved. Go into any good library, and there, indexed under decision making, are at least a score of recent books subindexed to science, engineering, business, ecology, public administration, educational administration, and a number of other subclassifications. The largest number of these are related to the field of management.

In books such as Arnold J. Meltsner's *Policy Analysis in the Bureaucracy* (1976) and Allan W. Lerner's *The Politics of Decision-Making* (1976), one finds some rather cogent observations relating to the problem being considered. To go into the whole philosophy underlying this resurging interest in decision would carry this study too far afield. However, one can suggest some ideas deserving fuller study and contemplation.

Decision is rarely, if ever, a completely isolated event because it has a past and a future. It is related to something else, from whether the widow with four children should buy lettuce or cornmeal with her few remaining pennies, to whether the United States should recognize mainland China or Taiwan (or both, if that were possible). Every lawyer recognizes this relativity factor. I recall that in my course on jurisprudence with Walter Wheeler Cook (whose reputation was in the conflict of laws), I was the unfortunate victim of his question, "Is there such a thing as pure fact?" I should have asked him to define "pure," of course! What I am saying about decision is a bit like that.

The more important lesson from recent research is that people in a bureaucracy tend to stop thinking and become merely victims of habit. When they are challenged they become uncomfortable, so they try to avoid challenges. To offset this lethargy, what does one do? Whether decision is by expert or administrator, the answer comes, "He tries to emphasize policy and innovation." In other words, instead of trying to find more difficult and time-consuming ways of doing the familiar, one turns to the equivalent of a good novel or a detective yarn for a change. Change the mental set and interest may go on growing. Stay in the rut and (if firing were not so difficult) the same person would be put out to pasture, like any old horse whose energies have failed.

"Once inside the encrusted and dark bureaucracy," says Meltsner, "the policy analyst sees himself as an intellectual with a flashlight of innovation. He thinks he is free to reflect and be a force for change" (p. 8). Or this:

> Not all the energy of the analyst goes into pushing ideas. Because there is a certain amount of pathology in the bureaucracy, expressed as an exaggerated concern for turf and personal aggrandizement, the policy analyst, like the bureaucrats, engages in a struggle for recognition, for status, and for reward (p. 9).

Another factor in decision making is negotiation. This is something at which the political leader is expert and hence the substantive, administrative expert needs to think in terms of reciprocal interchange of services and rewards with him if the program is to prosper. This is true, says Lerner, irrespective of whether the decision is an individual or an institutional one.

I cite these researches into the broader aspects of decision making as a means of reinforcing my criticisms of the underlying assumptions emerging from the *Morgan* decisions. Decision is so universal that it is neither judicial nor administrative, but both. Administrators are as likely to be as fair as judges, because in the last analysis the decisive factors are ones of character and personality. Is he competent? Is he objective? Is he resourceful and intelligent? If he is intelligent, he will realize that his decision relates to policy. He will recognize the policy factor openly in analyzing the alternatives that are available. But he will not legislate policy arbitrarily, if the authority to which to relate his interpretation is not there in the first place. He will not try to dominate the work of experts who happen to work in a related branch of government. Because he treats them with the respect he himself expects, he will not stoop to limit or restrict the expertise and discretion needed to do a professional job. Hence any idea of looking into the mind of another expert becomes offensive to him. His oath to support the Constitution disposes him toward wanting administrative experts to decide all the cases they can, so long as they do it competently and follow the law and the dual requirements of substantive and procedural due process.

But the administrator's process is not the process of the court or even of the law schools. It is the process that comes naturally and is congruent with the necessities of work in a different but related environment.

I have stated what I think is the statesmanlike view of complementary roles under the separation of powers because, unlike the great men in the field of law such as Cardozo, Frankfurter, Hand, Friendly, and a few others, there has been a tendency from time to time to overlook the fact that legal ethics apply to coworkers in other branches of the government. Their opposite, a meanness of mind, undoubtedly has been triggered in the past by the disturbing tendencies of the New Deal as they affected individuals and groups with conservative dispositions. But this neuroticism is scant justification for allowing nonethical considerations and a mean spirit to creep into the decisions and dicta of higher judicial tribunals.

What is needed is a commonsense view of what is involved in decision making. By this I mean fairness and not rule, because the former is a better guideline than the latter. Let me illustrate this from my own experience.

Immigration is a field that needs to be watched closely to assure fair play. There must be no second-class citizens. Everyone, irrespective of color, origin, or economic status, must be assured equal rights. Accordingly, when I discovered that the statutory law of Congress in 1938, when I took office, required the Secretary of Labor to decide personally and sign every exclusion or deportation decision coming from Immigration inspectors and boards, I took immediate steps to correct such an absurd situation. Every morning when I arrived at the office I would find a 12-foot table piled high with cases to be read, decided, and signed. My first step was to set up by executive order a Board of Immigration Appeals consisting of Immigration inspectors with power to decide. Then, since I still had the statutory authority to decide, I arranged to have an assistant who, in consultation with the chairman of the board, referred to my personal attention the difficult cases involving close decisions as they relate to law, fairness, and policy. The policy, as stated earlier, was to assure that everyone was treated with exact justice.

Later, when Immigration was transferred to Justice, I took an additional step. Again using the executive order, a provision was inserted under which if I was in doubt I could refer the case to the attorney-general for his review and decision. During the two-year period there were perhaps a half-dozen cases that were so referred. Meantime, in order to improve administrative due process, I had introduced the policy that no decision on administrative appeal could be reviewed by any Immigration inspector who had made the decision initially (that is, in the primary decision of the case). I further strengthened this policy by requiring that at the second review stage and before the case got to the Board of Immigration Appeals there should be a collegial decision by three inspectors instead of the original one. This was modeled after the method used in the U.S. Circuit Court of Appeals decisions.

So this was the hierarchy of decision making that seemed fair in every respect. As far as I could see, this system of administrative review and decision was as fair and as thorough as anything found in judicial justice, that is, the system of constitutional courts. But on top of this, any case still could be taken to a constitutional court, and some were.

I cite this experience because I believe that even in a sensitive area such as human rights that it is a better model than the system of hearing examiners and administrative law judges that has been introduced following the passage of the Administrative Procedure Act and amendments. All this I have been reporting was done without disrupting the even flow of operations in an action agency. It did not shatter and weaken the flow of administration: it strengthened it and improved fairness at the same time.

There are certain other agencies that need to be carefully scrutinized to assure the exact equivalent of judicial justice. They are few in number but all are important. One area already has been mentioned, that of the issuance of licenses in Federal Communications Commission cases. I know from study of this area that opportunities exist for favoritism and undue influence in awarding, revoking, and renewing licenses if the objectivity of the deciders is not closely watched. I do not think this is true any more, however, in the case of the Interstate Commerce Commission, which regulates railroads and other forms of carriers. The need here is for strong administration, converting a lax and inefficient transportation system into a network comparing favorably with the best found in other countries such as Japan, Switzerland, and Germany. The Commission should be dejudicialized as fast as possible. As the 1971 report, *A New Regulatory Framework* recommended, the best way of accomplishing this would be to separate the positive planning function and the appeals function into separate agencies, one solely operational and the other solely quasi-judicial.

No two industry situations are exactly alike. The cloth should be cut to fit the need. Uniformity, which is a vice of the Administrative Procedure-type of legislation, should be avoided. By and large, the desirable formula is to group study, planning, and promotion under one organization and, if the need exists—and it does not in every instance—set up a hearing and deciding tribunal to deal with appeals.

Those who are now hearing examiners and administrative judges thus would become candidates for positions in the administrative justice tribunals created. But hearing examiners and administrative judges, as such, would be abolished in most agencies where they are now found and the burden of proof would be put upon those who contend that they are needed in exceptional instances.

If the major independent regulatory agencies were abolished, I would not shed a tear. In many cases they have become so judicialized that they act as a counterpropulsive force in a whole industry, such as railroads or airlines. There is no question that throughout the 100-year history of major regulation in the United States, it has proved difficult to recruit and retain commissioners who are as qualified as they need to be. In many cases the commissions have been industry dominated and hence were independent in name only. There is no question that so long as courts in the final analysis set allowable rates of return on the investment, that the rate of return is higher and safer than in comparable competitive industries.

I doubt whether this singular feature of U.S. government will be substantially altered during my lifetime. True, other countries either do not use this device or, like England, have tried it and given it up. But I predict that we will continue to use the independent regulatory agencies, or IRAs (as they are called) for some additional time, and this for two reasons. First, although regulated industries sometimes grumble about bureaucracy and red tape, when it comes to a showdown they like the rate of return on the investment, and think that the only alternative is socialism. Second, the legal profession—and especially the organized lawyers who specialize in various areas of major regulation—have a good thing going, financially and otherwise. The commission device encourages contentiousness; the organization of commissions leads to long delays; and the judicialization and dominance of rule making make it possible to draw substantial legal fees from a single case that may run ten years or more. It is one of the best moneymaking areas of law. Like a fiduciary, therefore, the regulatory bar in communities such as Washington, D.C. and elsewhere have every reason to protect their property from outside tinkering of any kind. The best way to guarantee this is to use their influence inside the American Bar Association and other bar associations in the major cities of the country.

I am not so naive as to think that most of the judicialization and hamstringing of administration complained of in these pages as a spontaneous response of the rank and file of the American bar. Nor do I think that the leaders of the bar are necessarily reactionary in terms of economic policy. The excesses of the judicialization movement were directly traceable to the law firms—largely Washington law firms—that specialized in regulatory cases.

I have emphasized the collegial decision in the independent regulatory commissions and my Immigration experience as much as I have because these illustrations underscore the inconsistency of viewpoint and motivation found in the legal circles that successfully engineered the judicialization of administration. Would they recommend that decisions of the Supreme Court of the United States be converted into the decision of a single justice? If this had been the practice from the beginning, it seems likely that there would have been more than one war between the states. There is more wisdom in a collegial than in a one-judge decision, especially in an area such as constitutional and administrative law, where policy, political wisdom, and experience are bound to play so large a part in crucial cases. The *Morgan* holdings and dicta could be reversed, for example, as many another precedent has been in recent years. I think this is a necessary and salutary safety valve, and that those who try to treat these public law areas as if they were mechanical jurisprudence do themselves and others a disservice.

Nowhere is the unitary nature of the administrative process better illustrated than in the collective decision. When administration is allowed to be unified and coordinated, as explained in Chapter 3, the whole resources of the department and agency can be drawn upon, making a better decision. To try to isolate decision making within the agency, as the present system of hearing officers and examiners attempts to do, one then has to pass rules to prevent these isolated individuals from conferring with knowledgeable officials in the same agency—not in all respects, but in some.

In Immigration, we found that our inspectors who specialized in Chinese cases were the most prejudiced of all. Many claims to U.S. citizenship were based upon an alleged father's visit to mainland China and often the claim of parenthood was false. Over a period of time, therefore, these inspectors came to think that all Chinese were prevaricators. This was corrected by using the entire resources of the department, including training, reassignment, collegial reviews, and bringing in fresh personnel. In an isolated, single-judge decision this is more difficult to arrange. Moreover, if the administrative judge happens to dislike Chinese for some reason, the agency policy of fairness is an uphill fight all the way.

This danger is greatly exacerbated because of a common human failing: the top administrator comes to have a feeling of false security simply because of the charisma of the term "judge." Hence, over a period of time he does the easy thing instead of the gutsy thing. He rubber-stamps the decision of the examiner or the administrative judge on the rationalization that this allows him to spend more time elsewhere in management. If he were thinking clearly, as he must in a unified operation, he would realize that every unchallenged precedent sets the pattern for future policy. This is why Musolf, in a previous quotation, says that in effect the judge increasingly becomes the dominant influence in policy and not the top echelon of administrators. This may serve the temporary advantage of some client interest, such as the patriotic organization or the public utility stockholder, but it is injurious in the longer run to the citizens and their representative system of government. In areas such as Immigration, the common people frequently have a deeper and fairer sense of justice than the powerholders who seek some temporary advantage.

Fortunately, legal sociologists have begun to make intensive studies of the effects of judicializing the administrative process, and these studies deserve the careful perusal of the leaders of the American bar. Such a study is one by Philippe Nonet called *Administrative Justice: Advocacy and Change in a Government Department* (1969). Phillip Selznick, in his "Introduction," says that this study of an agency of public welfare (IAC) reveals that the agency changed its character as it judicialized. But, it would have kept its character and purpose under stronger administrative leadership.

In his study, Nonet also found that critics of the welfare state use judicialization as a cover to attack extensions of government (p. 3). The cumulative effect of judicialization results in "administrative withdrawal." After the bar took over, there was a retreat from administrative responsibilities; the commission progressively renounced its power and repudiated policy commitments set by the legislature. By the end of the evolution the agency had lost all of the major functions it had previously exercised. These consisted of such things as control, surveillance, education, assistance, and the initiation of new policies (p. 125). The agency lost its autonomy. It gravitated from initiative to passivity and from public welfare to private interests (p. 154). Nonet explains that administrative withdrawal and judicialization are inextricably related. As administrative action declines, there is progressive contentiousness, the substitution of formalization for informal processes, and the process reaches its inevitable outcome when adjudication completely supersedes administration (pp. 166, 198, 201). Further, routinization accompanies judicialization. Adjudication is nothing more than the flight from policy (p. 244). In short, the judicialization of workmen's compensation, says Nonet, resulted in the "privitization" of welfare claims that was the complete opposite of the intent of the legislature, whose original motivation was to escape from the common law rules that were considered socially objectionable (p. 261). Nonet therefore concludes that lawyers and their professional associations should begin to recognize that legalism and judicialization raise serious doubts concerning "the competence of the law as an instrument of problem-solving" (p. 365).

The tide has begun to turn. Even the American Bar Association is beginning to be worried about what initially seemed to be a good thing being carried to excess. Writing on "the functional limits of legality," Jeffery Lowell in *Law and Bureaucracy* (1975) points out that adjudication is appropriate for solving certain kinds of problems, but fails when attempts are made to utilize it as a substitute for administration. For one thing, judicialization militates against planning. Rules are for "like" situations— they cannot foresee the future. Rules are therefore unsuited to the guidance of situations where the activity is nonrecurring or unique (p. 135). Certain tasks are simply not amenable to rule and adjudication as lawyers characteristically use these terms (p. 155).

It is difficult to know the exact time at which the tide began to turn, but it was quite apparent by 1975. In this year alone, the Columbia, Yale, and Harvard law reviews published articles on administrative law in relation to public administration that deserve to be called statesmanlike. In the *Columbia Law Review*, Ernest Gellhorn and Glen O. Robinson raise the question, "What is administrative law?," and answer this by saying that "the time has come to recognize how small a part of the legal universe it embraces," concluding that an alternative in the form of a broad approach to "administrative government" may be the better solution. In the *Yale Law Journal*, in an article again exhibiting an appreciation of a broader grasp of political and social policy, Lloyd N. Cutler and David R. Johnson wrote on "regulation and the political process," suggesting that a key may be renewed attention to the issue of political responsibility in administrative policy making, and suggesting, inter alia, congressional authorization of procedurally restricted presidential directives to regulatory commissions. An article by Robert B. Stewart in the *Harvard Law Review* is called "the Reformation of Administrative Law," and this examines the possibility of interest group representation as a possible basis for the political process of decision making in administration. These articles illustrate the swing of the pendulum from an austere legalism to the resurgence of the political science orientation of early pioneers such as Frank J. Goodnow and Ernst Freund.

This chapter has attempted to show that deciding is universal and adjudication is not. Also, even when it comes to important decisions, results are frequently better when they are institutional and make use of the entire resources of the agency and government. There is no magic in simply calling a lawyer a judge and elevating him to a position where he either challenges or transcends the authority and responsibility that the executive head of an agency ought to have if a program is going to prove socially effective. Administration needs dynamism and vitality, not rigid rules and encouragements of bureaucracy.

What is needed is a fresh start, getting back to the greater freedom found a generation ago. The Administrative Procedure Act, with amendments, should be replaced by an agency-by-agency reexamination of decision making appropriate to that area of national life. Some forms of regulation are emerging, others are old and anemic. No standard solution can possibly hope to deal adequately with situations so diverse.

Instead of assuming that judicialization of administration is the universal goal, the policy of bar associations should be to put the burden of proof in each jurisdictional area on those who favor more judicialization rather than less. Accompanying this should be renewed attention to training and recruiting executives who, because of their personal traits, have as much claim to competence and fairness as justices of courts of law. As Redford says, the emphasis should be shifted to policy and political responsibility.

The trappings of the 1946 reform ought to be carefully reexamined. Administrative judges are needed outside the agencies for review purposes, for example, but it is a mistake to give them so much power without responsibility inside the agencies themselves. The Administrative Conference should either be replaced or its function should be broadened so as not to be obsessive about procedure (in the lawyer's sense) and with writing manuals of procedure for administrative judges. It would probably be better to abolish it and start over again.

Condemnation of regulation abounds, says Redford in "Regulation Revisited," while at the same time regulation expands every year into new fields. It is time to conclude, therefore, that regulation is here to stay and that if it is ever to be made effective and agreeable, it needs to be dealt with as part of the political process, with its values and lessons from the past constantly in mind.

NOTES

1. Lloyd D. Musolf, *Federal Examiners and the Conflict of Law and Administration* (Baltimore: Johns Hopkins University Press, 1952), chap. 3.

2. Emmette S. Redford, "Regulation Revisited," *Administrative Law Review* 28 (Summer 1976): 543–68.

3. Kenneth Davis, *Administrative Law and Government* (St. Paul: West Publishing, 1960), p. 215.

4. For an account of the "extraordinary sequence of public pronouncements" following the second *Morgan* case, see Walter Gellhorn, *Administrative Law: Cases and Comments*, (Chicago: Foundation Press, 1940), pp. 715–19.

5. Marshall E. Dimock, *Administrative Vitality: The Conflict with Bureaucracy* (New York: Harper & Row, 1959), chap. 8.

— *11* —

ADMINISTRATIVE DISCRETION

The conflict between the legal profession and the management profession over the range of permissible discretion is the most celebrated of all the issues separating them. Private management figures in this to some extent, as when it objects to certain kinds of government regulation restricting its freedom, but public administration bears the brunt of the burden. In the public sector it is hardly an exaggeration to say that administrators constantly complain either against the judiciary for attempting to strip managers of the freedom and choice that they think they need, or against the legal profession as a whole. They argue that due to the influence of lawyers they are bound in lilliputian threads of red tape and procedure to the point where they can accomplish very little and hence have little exhilaration in their work.

There are a number of reasons, largely historical, why discretion always has figured so prominently in the running battle between lawyers and administrators. The main one, of course, is that some lawyers think law consists wholly of rules, whereas it is hard to find any administrator who subscribes to this notion. If pushed into a corner where he has no choice but to define, the administrator would probably say that law, if it performs its true function, is an instrument of social change; at least so it seems to him from where he stands.

Historically, since both law and government grew out of monarchy and the class system, it would have been surprising if, early in the history of the common law (the civil law, too, for that matter) the idea had not grown up that the sovereign has discretion and his ministers must do strictly as they are told. Similarly with the class structure: the clerics and the landed gentry could have more freedom than the burghers or the king's servants because the former occupied a higher status and hence were considered right, when the latter were merely supposed to be dutiful servants. This residue of the past even affects traditionalists' attitudes toward representative assemblies. As pointed out in Chapter 8, there is still alive in both the United Kingdom and the United States, among conservative jurists and judges, the idea that for some occult reason the law is to be trusted and popular assemblies are not, even when the constitution says that Parliament is paramount, as in England. This residual attitude is due in some part to the idea that the privileged classes are to be trusted and the common people are not.

In this comparison, the courts are equated with the conservative classes, while the popular assembly still conjures up images of Cromwell. Similarly, when one thinks of the professional civil service one thinks of the nineteenth-century substitute for the leadership previously provided for centuries by the members of the king's household—all of them noblemen—who became the heads of what are now government departments. Before today's citizen can fully trust the modern public administrator, he must first remove from his mind the residue of prejudice that causes him to think that judges can be trusted but that top civil servants cannot.

There is the additional factor that if government is not to be trusted and is continually corrupted by amoral pressure groups seeking only their own ends, no one in government is to be trusted, not even the judges. This is a false reading of the facts. In country after country the professional civil service is the single most dedicated aggregation of any in the country. When subversion from either extreme threatens to overthrow constitutional government, it has been they—not the judges or the military—who have held the country to its constitutional moorings. A good example of this is Turkey, where I represented the United Nations in 1953–54, when the Ataturk reforms were threatened by reactionaries.

Previous chapters already have suggested the main reason why discretion is so essential to effective administration. It is because freedom to choose between alternative solutions is essential to problem solving. The interest groups and the legislature analyze the fabric of society constantly to determine the main lines of policy whereby vexing social problems such as crime and inflation can be cured; but if any of these policies is to succeed, the administrators have prime responsibility for supplying the know-how and organizational skills to accomplish the social purpose. This is true under any form of government: monarchy, aristocracy, popular government, and even dictatorship. In one-man or one-class rule, the power wielder may subdue the rank and file with the threat of police or troops, but if the regime is to attempt to better the lot of the people by building roads, distributing the mails, or providing water and fertilizer for agriculture and industry, it is only the administrator who can assure that these things will be accomplished.

The history of the term discretion tends to confirm the thesis being argued here. The two English words, "discrete" and "discreet" have a common root. They mean to "distinguish" one thing from another. Hence the word discrete has come to mean "distinct," while discreet connotes discernment, judiciousness, circumspection, and caution. Similarly, the key term discretion also derives from the idea of making distinctions, while later it came to mean discernment to distinguish. So construed, the term discretion was interpreted as meaning to judge. At this point, whether it was literally a judge or an administrator, the common meaning was that of having the liberty to decide or to act according to one's best judgment.

Philosophers are almost uniformly agreed that judgment is the highest personal qualification of the administrator. Having said this, it is found that judgment is described by the dictionary as the quality of the prudent or sagacious individual.

These are the linkages. If the individual is sagacious and prudent he is to be trusted. This trust takes the form of allowing him enough liberty to make the choices that his expertness, wisdom, and sound judgment entitle him to make because he has the necessary traits of character.

The inference is clear: if a person is trustworthy he must be trusted. If he is not trusted by an act of delegation from higher authority, two things are obvious: he will not be permitted to use his potential and will become frustrated and lethargic; second, if he is not given this delegated authority, society itself will be the loser. This may sound like an ode to the administrator, but it is far from that: the tribute is to liberty and not to any individual.

Perhaps some examples of discretion in action will make my point even better than relying upon more history of philosophical analysis.

When we were setting up the Recruitment and Manning Organization of War Shipping during World War II, we wanted to pay a division head $6,500 (which was then considered a good salary), and were told by the classification people in Civil Service that we could have two officials at $5,600 apiece but that we could not have one at

$6500. They didn't object to the salary, thought the responsibility justified the amount, but said quite frankly that the figure did not accord with their preconceived notion of how we should organize. "But I don't *want* two people," I objected, "I want to keep my organization small and hard hitting." I also argued that my solution would save the taxpayer $4,700 a year and that the country would get more for its money with a single official. But they persisted. Finally I had to appeal all the way to the top of the commission—to the three presidential appointees—where my discretion was at least supported. This is not an exceptional case. Civil Service legalists have their attachments to rules, as do others.

In another example, the biggest problem we faced in the early days of World War II was the sitdown strike of Chinese seamen on Allied ships in New York harbor. They wanted the same pay as whites. Under U.S. law we could have thrown all of them in jail for three months, as other Allied countries were doing. After consulting my congressional committee as well as my superiors in the executive branch, we decided we would not do this. Instead, we insisted on the principle of equal pay for equal work, and backed this up by telling our Allies that we would not give them new Liberty ships unless they agreed to support this policy. They eventually did, and after that there were no more sitdown strikes during the ensuing period of hostilities.

We exercised a discretion. We had authority to put all these strikers in jail for three months. Did we take the law into our own hands by not doing so? That is one possible interpretation of our actions. Our discretionary view was that justice and law are one and the same thing and so long as we did not actually go contrary to the existing provisions of the law, we had a legitimate administrative discretion. Our discretion was never disputed in the courts, but perhaps it would have been in peacetime.

In both of these illustrations—and in others like them that grow out of experience—there were objectives of policy and administration that transcended the decision in the particular case. In the first illustration, we thought that to help win the war we needed a small, hard-hitting organization, and we were willing to fight for it. We had just turned over the recreation and welfare end of our program to a private organization, the United Seamen's Service, because we did not want to double our congressional appropriation and double the size of our personnel. Of necessity we operated from Sydney to Murmansk, as it was, because wherever the war went we had to be first on the spot.

In the second illustration, our concern was for the morale of our own merchant marine and the millions of aliens and citizens who believed that morale standards should not be lowered, even in wartime. It was a moral decision, but many of the best opinions of courts have been of this kind. Being administrators, we knew that there is always a close connection between moral and morale, and morale wins wars, in peacetime as well as during periods of national crisis.

The point is that the skillful administrator must look into the fabric of society and judge where the country is going and what is just. In any realistic interpretation of the law, everyone who has a responsibility for law should do this, too, but not if the law prohibits the contemplated move. Then the law should be changed before the action is taken. As long as there is sufficient discretion, the possibility of fashioning a distinctive solution is present. This can do no conceivable harm so long as the distinctions are prudent and sound. Perhaps the definition of discretion I like best is "propriety of behavior."

We come back again to the idea that the essence of good administration is aplomb, the feeling, backed by facts, that the administrator is on top of the job and is able to direct the entire proceeding with grace and a sense of unity. Once his necessary discretions are interfered with for any except just cause, his strategy and his self-confidence begin to collapse.

Viewed as a national asset, discretion occupies such an important place in law and administration that it has no equal. This is one of the reasons why as a matter of constitutional doctrine the judiciary in the United States will not interfere with a political question. A political question is not merely a matter of avoiding partisanship; it is also assurance that "the will of the state" (as it used to be called) shall be guaranteed success in such vital areas as diplomacy, the making of public policy, and anything involving survival.

James Hart, in his *Administrative Law* (1950), states this doctrine very well: ". . . the courts recognize the *widest* discretion in the Executive in its exercise of 'political' questions like the recognition of a foreign government . . ." (p. 662). Hart then goes on to explain, more widely, that discretion involves choice, and that the governing statute may vest in the administrator the competence to make such a choice. "In this event," says Hart, "it is generally conceded that upon judicial review the courts do not have the competence to overturn the choice which has been made." Choice, however, does not involve arbitrary choice. Moreover, the writ of mandamus has long been used to enforce a specific ministerial duty in which a certain act is provided for in specific statutory provisions (p. 662).

Lest this principle of judicial construction be misunderstood, however, it is important to distinguish between acts that are mandatory under a statute, such as imposing a fine or requiring a certain kind of action, and the larger, and different, question of not interfering with the strategy and flow of work that is the administrator's birthright. There are some things in administration that are scientific and that represent "the one best method," but these have a specific character; they are factors that may be quantified and measured. As such, they are more easily evaluated and assessed against an absolute scale. Except for this, however, which the engineer Frederick Taylor made much of, administration in its larger ranges is not a science but a strategy. In acting on any strategy, whether in diplomacy or war, the number of variables, and hence of alternative strategies and choices, are found at all levels of administration, tending to become greater the nearer the apex at which the decisions are made. It is this distinction, which is often overlooked by lawyers when they think about administration, that is a major explanation of why bar associations, even with the best of intentions, have attempted to standardize what should not be standardized and have treated the so-called administrative process as if it were a problem in mathematics.

Higher (strategy) administration subscribes to the adage, "There are many ways to skin a cat." The two examples I gave earlier are examples of this. Take a common illustration: you can throw the book at individuals and associations, as in an antitrust suit, or you can counsel and advise and attempt to get voluntary compliance. So long as the administrator has the necessary discretion, one method may be tried at one time and the other at another time, and neither is necessarily superior because one may succeed at one time and the other at another. Eventually, of course, both may have to be used if progress toward the social goal of the legislation is to be achieved.

The goal that certain jurists have had in the past, namely, to remove all discretion from law, is pernicious in the extreme. Fortunately, as law has become socialized, there is now a wider awareness that discretion is on a par with law. The two are complementary, not antagonistic. So long as the standard is clear and the courts can step in at any time to enforce, by mandamus, a ministerial act, as defined above, that is adequate safeguard.

As a result, in courses on administrative law much less is heard nowadays than formerly about the sharp dividing line between ministerial and discretionary power. As suggested earlier, the distinction was long colored by the social assumptions of a bygone age. I recall that as a student of Goodnow's in administrative law between 1925 and 1928, he seemed to delight in assigning me cases on ministerial power for oral report. I think he felt then, as I did, that the distinction between ministerial and discretionary decisions had been overly refined by the courts.

When in *The Frontiers of Public Administration* (1936) I wrote a piece on "The Role of Discretion in Modern Administration," I had already learned that discretion is more essential in certain areas of government than in others. In addition to the political question, there are at least five other categories where the requirements are special in each case. One of these is crisis situations such as war, depression, inflation, or martial law. Here all possible dispatch is necessary, and therefore the administrator needs resiliency and contrivance. A second is in summary jurisdictions involving such things as public health and the abatement of nuisances. A third, which has grown immensely since 1936, is the field of licensing and inspections, one of Freund's favorite themes. A fourth is major regulation such as that represented by the regulatory tribunals, which has been the favorite theme of courses on administrative law in recent years. The fifth is routine administration as found at all levels.

All of these categories have one thing in common: everyone in administration needs to think in terms of alternatives of choice or little intelligence will be used and little progress will be made toward solving pressing social problems. Administrators are, above all else, problem solvers, and it is common experience that if one does not experiment and innovate, solutions will be hard to find.

The big problem confronting the United States now, as Mr. Chief Justice Burger is constantly reminding us, is to find workable substitutes for excessive contentiousness and the overburdening of courts. As Burger said in an address to the American Bar Association at Columbia University on May 27, 1977, law in its broadest sense is not an end in itself: it is a tool, a means to an end. That end is justice, as nearly as fallible humans can achieve it, for people and their problems. One must not exalt the means at the expense of the ends. Complex procedures, refined and developed for certain types of more complex cases, are inappropriate and even counterproductive when applied to the resolution of the kinds of disputes that are the focus of attention today.

A move in the direction of finding administrative substitutes for an overburdened judiciary cannot be long delayed. It will take the form of arbitration, conciliation, bankruptcy proceedings; center in such areas as landlord-tenant disputes, fraud and consumer claims proceedings, insurance claims, ecology cases, family relations, even estates and wills. The thing they will all have in common is that the administrative model rather than the formal judicial model will need to be relied upon. Hence, to revert to what was said earlier in introducing this subject, if discretion is discernment and judging, administrative resources need to be mobilized for the added burdens that lie ahead.

In a tribute to W. W. Willoughby called "A Scientific Approach to the Study of Law," Walter Wheeler Cook, although he wrote in 1937, was prophetic in saying that it is preposterous to suppose that remedying the known evils accompanying civil procedures can ever be made satisfactory merely by simplifying these procedures and making them more efficient. The way out, said Cook, is to be found in two alternatives: either judicial self-government on the part of industry and business, or the development of specialized administrative tribunals taking the load off the courts. In the latter case, the political state would create the special tribunals, while in the case of industry and commerce, the self-government would have to operate under the supervision of the state. We have been too practical, said Cook; now we need to be inventive and resourceful.[1]

How do the views expressed in this chapter accord with those of Kenneth Davis in his 1969 lectures at Louisiana State University, *Discretionary Justice: A Preliminary Inquiry*? Before turning to the answer to this question, let it be said that Davis's painstaking research is justifiably called brilliant, and this book should be required reading wherever public administration and administrative law are taught. The book consists of eight chapters that suggest its content: the what and the why of discretion, the rule of law and the nondelegation doctrine, confining discretion, structuring discretion, checking discretion, selective enforcement and privilege, confining, structuring, and checking the prosecuting power, and summary and perspective. As will be appreciated from this outline, Davis deals with a broad area, the whole of government: legislatures, courts, criminal and civil cases, the prosecutory function, and administration in the ordinary sense. The book also makes use of foreign experience as well, and Davis uses this knowledge to suggest possible improvements in how the United States handles certain problems. In effect, it is a long essay on the role of discretion in all of government—federal, state, and local—making it more difficult to evaluate and compare his treatment of the purely administrative.

His treatment of criminal law and prosecution is the pithiest illustration of his thesis. Also, he says some wise and penetrating things about law making, rule making, and administrative adjudication. It would not be unfair to say that in *Discretionary Justice*, Davis provides the capstone for all the wisdom he has collected over the years as a result of close observation of government in action, a fitting summation of his 12 volumes and more than 60 articles published before 1969.

Davis thinks that discretion does not begin where law ends. Instead he finds it is essential, an integral part of law. His main concern is to see that it is neither too little nor too much. If discretion is to be kept in balance it must be brought out into the open and be structured, as well as checked. He denies that discretion is something intangible that cannot be rationally understood and assessed, and hence his main object is to make it better understood and make a better tool for serving both private and public interest. He objects to the idea that law is merely rules, and in so doing subscribes to the functional, evolutionary philosophy of law expressed in these pages. In short, I am in fundamental agreement with his main positions and find him fair and middle-of-the-road in everything he says. Davis never hesitates to speak his mind. Quite justly, in a concluding note (p. 233, Illini edition, 1971) he criticizes the modern tendency of political scientists to fail to express opinions, especially when they are based upon intensive research.

In defining discretion, Davis goes further than I have because he introduces a qualifying phrase that begs the question: "A public officer has discretion whenever *the effective limits of his power* leave him free to make a choice among possible courses of action or *inaction*" (p. 4). My reservations have to do with the *underlined* words. It seems simpler to define discretion as choice and then explain the caveats and conditions afterward. Also, I do not think that inaction should be a part of the definition, although the matter is so important that I am glad Davis stresses it throughout his lectures as much as he does.

Davis's reason for including the effective limits on the administrator's power is forthright, if not convincing. A good deal of discretion, says Davis, is "illegal and of questionable legality" (p. 4). To me, this calls for a conclusion of fact and should not be included in the definition. If it is "really" illegal, the illegality in some instances may be attributable to something other than discretion.

My next disagreement is that Davis states that discretion is explained by three factors: facts, values, and influences. From this he generalizes, "most discretionary decisions are intuitive" (p. 5). I have two main difficulties with this. The first is that more than these three elements are involved in discretionary acts. The most important is the one mentioned earlier—the grand strategy of the administrator and his need to synthesize all elements into an effective whole. I think Davis senses this need more clearly than do most writers on administrative law, but nowhere does he state it specifically. Moreover, it seems clear that there are other factors worthy of mention that should be included in Davis's three-pronged list of elements. One of these is expertise. Another, closely related thereto, is what Chester Barnard (as noted in an earlier chapter) calls the synthesizing quality of mind that distinguishes the experienced executive's mental pattern. A third is what Mary Parker Follet called "the law of the situation." By this she meant that the context of the decision, or the act, determines what constitutes the appropriate (almost inevitable) response. One turns not only to social psychology but also to engineering and science for validation of this premise.

I also object to Davis saying that most discretion is simply intuitive. This is contrary to his main thesis, namely, that discretion can be rationally understood and that it is high time that it was. I would agree with him, however, if all he means is that integrative factors such as I have been mentioning are usually involved in discretionary decisions. What I suspect is that this observation fits in with his statement that much discretion is "illegal and of questionable legality," whereas Davis wants to make everything "open." I think there is a confusion of terms here. I agree that discretions should be "open and above-board," but that is a different thing than saying that a court (or even a psychiatrist) can, and should, attempt to pry into the mind of the administrator to see how the right and left lobes of the brain are interacting. I agree with Brandeis's remark about letting the sunlight in, but this is different from saying that everything that cannot be isolated or quantified is patently illegal. One is in an area where everything cannot be isolated and counted, and I see no compelling reason why one should try.

My major disagreement with Davis, however, has to do with his main thesis, which again is threefold (p. 15). First, much discretionary justice that is not governed by or guided by rules should be. I think there are too many rules already. If Davis had said "standards" or "policy," and if "guided by" is what he meant, I could agree with him. But if his statement is taken literally, then I think there are some areas, such as police (which Davis gives a great deal of attention to) where his generalization applies, but that this field-by-field treatment is the way to handle the matter instead of generalizing. His second proposition is that much discretionary justice is without rules because no one knows how to formulate rules. I should have preferred to say that there are some instances, which Davis mentions, where this may be true, but that as a sweeping generalization it is exaggerated and demeaning to the competence found in most government offices. Finally, Davis's third observation is that discretionary justice is without rules because discretion is preferred to rules that may be formulated, and that individualized justice is often better. I think so, too. If justice is discreet, reasoned, and prudent, why shouldn't it be considered preferable to more rules? As for the second part of this proposition, the whole idea of common law is that justice is individualized, treated case-by-case.

Now one comes to an excellent summary of position where I am much happier because I can applaud almost everything Davis says:

> 1. Discretion, as a tool, is our principal source of creativeness in government and in law. "Rules, alone, untempered by discretion, cannot cope with the complexities of modern government and of modern justice." Yet every truth extolling justice may be matched by a truth concerning its dangers.
>
> 2. One should not oppose discretionary power, but only unnecessary power [unnecessary, of course, is a mendicant word]. Let us not oppose discretionary power *commensurate with the tasks undertaken by government* [this I like, particularly], but let us oppose discretionary power that outruns these tasks.
>
> 3. Let us not oppose discretionary justice that is properly confined, structured, and checked; let us oppose discretionary justice that is the opposite of these (pp. 25–26).

I suppose that of these three—confined, structured, and checked—I might be more sympathetic to the middle term, structured, and less enthusiastic about the other two, confined and checked, until they are more carefully defined. Davis also says somewhere that he is suspicious of emotion in exercising discretion. If you are going to consider values as a main factor, as Davis does, I wonder if you ought to try to eliminate what our forebears called the moral sentiments. One can have feelings and still be rational and fair. I learned this daily in Immigration.

In his summary chapter Davis comes to two conclusions that I disagree with strongly and one that I applaud. The first reads, "Improved statutory standards [are] largely a false hope." I have the feeling, perhaps unjustified, that in saying this Davis is trying to underscore the importance of his own solution, rulemaking, by casting doubt on the solution that Freund and others thought most promising. Be that as it may, the three reasons Davis gives for denigrating better bill drafting are not impressive: he doubts most legislatures' ability to create better standards; standards do not reach the problems he has been emphasizing; and third, the real hope for the future lies in wider and more effective use of administrative rule making (p. 217). I think he is wrong about this.

Davis's second main conclusion with which I disagree is his recommendation that rule making be made more elaborate and that procedure be spelled out more fully than it is even now in the Administrative Procedure Act (p. 219). I think Davis is dead wrong about this. Moreover, there is strong indication that the American Bar Association is beginning to think that the Administrative Procedure Act has been carried to excess. Davis hooks this conclusion to the one just mentioned—his disillusionment with legislatures. I think it is a higher act of statesmanship to try to improve legislative bill drafting and administrative justice at all its focal points, rather than single out one area (rule making) for what seems to me excessive emphasis.

Where I do applaud Davis's recommendations is in his frequent reference to selective and privileged enforcement of the law, especially in police jurisdictions, where much law and policy are made. I do not think this is so much a matter of discretion, however, as lack of other necessary administrative tools, such as better training and better supervision and control.

In conclusion, one of the best features of Davis's book is that he provides a wealth of illustrations of discretion at work. I call the reader's attention especially to pages 9, 34, and 82. I agree with him also that a great deal of intensive research is needed on discretion before one can be as sure of one's ground as necessary. Being an admirer of Davis, let me end on this positive note (out of context, to be sure, but hopefully not misleading): "A rule is undesirable when discretion will serve better" (p. 54), and

> Inventing rules to answer all regulatory questions is far beyond the intellectual capacity of the ablest men. Rules are essential, but discretion is also essential—and the right mixtures of rules and discretion. Our objective should be to find for each case or each problem the right proportion of rule and discretion (p. 42).

In 1976, however, when Davis published his *Discretionary Justice in Europe and America*, he apparently had become convinced that administrative procedure legislation is something of a holy cause. Davis makes it plain in his closing chapter, in a section called "Unreviewed Discretionary Action in Europe" (pp. 197–203), that "the quality of justice in administrative courts is high," and that by and large the European countries he and his colleagues surveyed are quite content with their administrative performance. One would have thought therefore that the burden of proof for recommending the U.S. type of administrative procedure legislation would have depended upon a demonstrated need. Instead, Davis merely takes the need for granted. He seems to assume that because the United States regiments administrative procedure, everyone else should do likewise. My reading of the same facts is that we ought to mend our ways because European results are so much better than those we have produced since 1946. I wish Davis had confined himself to his main recommendation, namely, correcting the uncontrolled discretion of prosecutors in the United States (p. 193), because I am sure he is right in this. Also, no one can take issue with his admonition that Europeans ought to study the interna of administrative action for fuller and more complete insights. But to recommend the U.S. system when the European one is superior is not a clear and objective reading of the evidence.

When searching to see how other writers deal with the subject of discretion, one interesting discovery was that Bernard Schwartz, in the index to his 1977 edition of *Administrative Law*, has only these references to discretion: See Availability of Review; Scope of Review; Tort Suits; Table of Statutes; Administrative Procedure Act (p. 722). From this I received confirmation of what social psychologists teach: ostracism is a frequently used weapon.

Others, often through case studies, have begun to dig more deeply into this vexing question of discretion. Such a study is Philippe Nonet's *Administrative Justice* (1969), which was mentioned in an earlier chapter. This study had to do with workmen's compensation and social welfare. Nonet says some pithy things:

> When discretion is transferred from the administrator to the judge, the latter invariably gets involved in policy. He cannot decide without committing himself (p. 255).

This may be a bit of an exaggeration, but there is a fundamental truth in what he says.

In one of Nonet's best insights into what actually occurs, he develops the thesis that because the administrator must deduce his rules from the law instead of the situation, his whole approach is colored. Hence the transformation of policies into rules restricts the administrator. Accordingly, this transformation gives the judicial system an advantage the administrative system does not have. The judicial system has the means of creating rules as well as implementing them; the administrative system does not have the same right. Nonet therefore concludes that if government as a whole is to keep its authority (and competence), it must be assured this same right (pp. 251–52).

Nonet also breaks new ground in pointing out that when judicialization occurs early in the game, before the administrator and the interested public have done what they need to do after the program has had more experience, two resulting restrictions of discretion have adverse effects: first, the narrower the discretion allowed, the less opportunity interested parties have to influence existing policies and substantive matters; and second, the inevitable result is that legal criticism is diverted away from substance and focuses almost completely on narrow procedural questions (p. 5). This is exacerbated further because, as pointed out in Chapter 7 above, the teaching of administrative law has come to focus almost entirely on procedural matters instead of on substantive ones. The effect is to negate the expertise of the administrator and leave substance in limbo.

In another full-length case study entitled *Law and Bureaucracy: Administrative Discretion and the Limits of Legal Action* (1975), Jeffrey L. Jowell probes deeply into the questions that have been considered here and writes an entire chapter on discretion and the politics of administration (Chapter 6). Jowell defines discretion in a manner that will be understood by the administrator but that is still somewhat foreign to the thinking of lawyers: discretion is "room for decisional manoeuvre possessed by a decision maker" (p. 156). Some may object to Jowell's use of the word manoeuvre, but it is clear from the context that what he means is what I have variously described as problem solving, administrative strategy, and flow of work. In other words, it is an attempt to combine substance and procedure in terms of larger social and legal objectives. Jowell is realistic in saying that discretion is rarely absent, rarely absolute, for it is always a matter of degree. It ranges along a continuum from high to low. When it is high there is more room to manoeuvre, when it is low it is because "rules do not allow much room for interpretation" (p. 156).

I also like the realistic way in which Jowell deals with the limits of rules, or what he calls "rule-governed conduct." A rule, he says, is a "general direction," applicable to a number of like situations that may arise in the future. Further, unless rules contain sufficient exceptions (and not invariably then), they cannot be tailored to unique, nonrecurring, or individual circumstances. When it is taken into account that, practically speaking, no two cases, even in the same area, are precisely alike—as both lawyers and administrators know— uniqueness, individuation, and problem solving suffer. An impersonal bureaucracy, producing personalized service and human characteristics, is something of a misnomer (p. 135). The higher on a scale organizations go toward rules, the more bureaucratic they must expect to become.

Possibly because Jowell spells maneouvre in the English way, I was reminded of a statement by Sir Leslie Scarman in his book, *English Law—The New Dimension* (1974), wherein this court of appeals judge remarks, "The illumination of obscurity and the process of first asking fresh questions has given the law and the judges *a degree of flexibility and the room for manoeuvre which in turn bring the gift of survival*" (p. 52, emphasis added). Hurrah! Presumably we all desire survival, and if manoeuvreability is the way to assure it, possibly we might come to favor that, too. But has anyone considered the desirability of according the administrator the same right?

I find the treatment of this subject by Ronald M. Dworkin, as found in Robert S. Summers (ed.), *Essays in Legal Philosophy* (1976), a fitting way of concluding these reflections on the issues of administrative discretion. Dworkin says it is the positivists who have created all the pother concerning this disputatious term: they have lifted it out of its context. Discretion, says Dworkin, is understood only when connected with its appropriate context. Otherwise it is "always colored by the background of understood information against which it is used" (p. 45). Dworkin then proceeds to describe the meanings of the term by reducing them to their weak and strong senses. In the weak sense, discretion may mean one of several things: the official must act mechanically and use no judgment; alternatively, an official may have final authority and cannot be reviewed or reversed by any other official. These are the two extremes and both qualify as weak.

What is a strong connotation of the term? This can be when an official is allowed to use judgment in applying standards set for him by someone else; he has finality because he has used judgment; or he may not be required to rely upon a particular standard because it is not relevant. In none of this does the official have what may be called license. Moreover, he is still open to criticism. All a strong discretion means is that within certain parameters the official is free to use his judgment and to act.

The legal positivists, says Dworkin, are not content to try to reduce everything to rule and strip others of their discretion. They next argue that if a case (or act) is not controlled by an established rule, the judge must decide it by exercising discretion (p. 47). In other words, it is all right for judges to exercise discretion, but administrators do not have an equal right. The extreme positivists even go so far as to contend that "judges always have discretion, even when a clear rule is in point, because the judges are ultimately the final arbiters of the law" (p. 47).

Dworkin believes that law consists of principles, not merely rules, and because of this he concludes that no judge is above principle and that administrators and judges ought to be regarded as on a plane of equality so long as they both abide by principles. He answers the objection that principles are not sufficiently clear by saying that they can be made clear enough, for all practical purposes, and that even if they were not as clear as rules, rules have a stultifying effect.

I agree with him, and I think most administrators do, too.

Finally, most lawyers seem to take it for granted that administrators have a natural disposition to abuse their powers. I doubt this very much, and I have worked among them during much of my life. But there is an aspect of this uninformed judgment that may be right. Administrators know that choice always involves the risk of being proved wrong. Hence, if they are to achieve outstanding social accomplishments, they sometimes have to take risks. If representative government is to succeed, an environment should be encouraged in which risk taking is regarded with approval.

Mortimer and Sanford Kadish deal with this question in their book, *Discretion to Disobey* (1975).[2] It is a careful, scholarly book and worth a close reading. These authors have invented the term "deviational discretion," by which they mean sometimes taking the risk of doing things in one's own way, while realizing that officials will be held accountable for their successes and failures (pp. 44–45). Believing, as Holmes did, that the life of the law is not logic, but experience:

> The law imposes order, and in an orderly way. But it may also admit the impulses of disorder in the shaping of its acts. In a partially disorderly way, ... the law may channel into its processes the beliefs, aspirations, and guesses both of those who make and apply its rules and of those obliged to obey them. The law itself accepts the challenges to legitimate departures from its own rules. Hence a system providing for the legitimation of rule departures reminds us again of an analogy between law and art: The development of one as of the other draws vitality from embracing within itself a random element. In sum, to the extent it is proper to speak of the law as a system, it now seems the sort of system that in the very process of its internal operations surrenders self-enclosure and completeness in order to accept, and capitalize on, influences from that outside milieu in which it is immersed (p. 218).

This is good legal thinking, it is even better administrative philosophy.

NOTES

1. Walter Wheeler Cook, "A Scientific Approach to the Study of Law," in *Essays in Political Science: In Honor of Westel Woodbury Willoughby*, ed. J. B. Mathews and J. Hart (Baltimore: Johns Hopkins University Press, 1937), pp. 226–27.

2. Mortimer R. and Sanford H. Kadish, *Discretion to Disobey: A Study of Lawful Departure From Legal Rules* (Palo Alto: Stanford University Press, 1973).

— *12* —

RECONCILIATION

The requirements of a competent government in the latter part of the twentieth century are these: (1) the government should focus on its indispensable functions that are required for survival; failure to do this is a main reason citizens have come to have such a low opinion of government at the present time; (2) the government should not attempt to do, by direct action, too much, or it will fail; (3) government therefore needs to arrange its priorities to assure that first things are reasonably well administered; (4) it must develop inventiveness to see that necessary things that can be delegated elsewhere are appropriately so delegated; (5) it should avoid concentrating too much authority at any one point in the hierarchy of power; (6) in limiting government's role to the optimal (workable) size, it should use the market system to the greatest possible extent; (7) government should assume that money and earned surplus are limited, as are resources, and be convinced that profligate expenditures eventually will cause collapse of free government; (8) it should cherish and strengthen the separation of powers while working just as hard to assure the necessary cooperation; (9) it needs a large and renewable supply of managers who can assure high-level production in a personnel system devoid of civil service mentality; and (10), it needs lawyers who are servants of the courts and guardians of the state instead of being manipulators for their own advantage.

What these propositions add up to is assuring responsibility for not wasting human, monetary, and productive resources, but husbanding them for use by future generations in an environment in which citizens respect values that have a universal quality. The end of government is the releasing of vital energies that will enable people to develop a satisfying way of life without resorting to violence, dishonesty, or subversion. Seen in this light, law is both a reflector of values and an instrument of orderly growth. Change is not an end in itself but only a means to balanced and free adjustments.

Constitutional government is a limited government, as the framers of the U.S. Constitution believed, but it should not be limited in effectiveness, which is the modern and mistaken view. Government should be limited only by being confined to those areas of activity that are needful at any given time, that are in accord with the moral principles expressed in laws and constitutions, and that cannot satisfactorily be devolved upon individuals and voluntary agencies for reasons previously suggested.

Rules should play only a minimal part in the operation of free government. They are used only as a last resort, and then sparingly. Other stronger and more cohesive substitutes for rules are ethical standards, common consent, voluntary initiative, private property, the market system, competence, the separation of powers, the delineation of roles, and checks and balances. These are all tied together by policy standards based upon openness, fairness, and workability. Government under law is a constant equation between what needs to be done urgently for the country as a whole and what is just and fair. Law, like everything else in government, is a socializing factor. A good discussion of some of these propositions is found in Chapter 9 of Charles Lindblom's recent book, *Politics and Markets* (1977).

When rules are too much relied upon, as they have been in the United States in recent times, the attempt always will result in failure. In an audacious attempt to control government by detailed rules limiting officials' authority, says Lindblom, frustration is the inevitable consequence. His suggested reason for this is that because everyone has a part in this, government is so complex, unpredictable, and has such ever changing ways that the attempt to reduce everything to rule is doomed to failure. And yet, stubbornly and irrationally, the attempt persists (p. 130). I agree with his conclusion, but am inclined to stress an additional and even more significant factor, namely, the tendency of the legal profession to ride roughshod over administrative competence and discretion, with resulting debilitation of institutional effectiveness.

Philosophically, I have refused to get caught up in the controversy over whether law is rules or principles, because it seems obvious to me that it is both. On balance, though, I do not much favor the legal positivist group, and this for a reason that has a special appeal to managers. Those who want to reduce everything to rules are pedants and perfectionists who do not realize that without the spice of life, existence would become unendurable. This ties in with what I said earlier about risk taking—nothing ventured, nothing gained. Psychologists tell us that the personality type that is determined to reduce everything to neatness and rules is an authoritarian personality. He suffers from fear and does not have sufficient self-confidence. Hence, in effect, when he tries to reduce life to rules he does so for two reasons: to build a protective wall around himself and to force others to do what he thinks is right, irrespective of whether they agree or not.

This same psychological explanation also applies to the collective behavior of the group. They are afraid of government, either because they have guilty consciences or because they are plain fearful. They figure that if they tie the government up in knots it will no longer be a threat. But as Sherlock Holmes might say, "They make one fatal mistake." They do not realize until it is too late that a government that has essential functions to perform and cannot discharge them as well as some rival form of government (such as communism) is already on a toboggan. Similarly, a government that does most things poorly becomes so incompetent that it attempts too much, wastes the national strength, causes a taxpayer revolt. Then, when the government is needed, as in a war or a depression, it takes months or years to rebuild people's confidence. This is what has happened in the United States: we have reviled government, and like a Greek god that was not quite dead, it has struck back at us and threatens to destroy us.

A second weakening factor is our personnel system, or lack of it. Forty years later, I am still marveling at the outpouring of talent that flowed into New Deal administration and World War II. Most of it was not trained in the managerial art, but some of these small-town individuals became the best managers. This does not surprise me. The greatest U.S. inventors and capitalists have started as mechanics and self-made men. The best military commanders are the ones who in peacetime do not like desk jobs. This is not to express an anti-intellectual bias. It is to suggest that certain kinds of training seem to dull the resourcefulness of self-made men and render them less effective than if they had not received that particular kind of training. In other words, training can hurt potential as well as draw it out. In some ways the apprenticeship method of induction into the law was preferable to the modern system, especially when the school is slapdash and has the wrong motivations. Similarly, many business-men and public administrators did a much better job when they used their native intelligence. Now they are expected to follow the book. They follow precedent and neglect to think. They do the socially approved thing and do not have the courage to take risks.

There is no question that this timidity of mind is attributable in large part to the negative, defensive orientation of the civil service and the legalistic, rule-ridden outlook of the legal profession. What they have in common is legalism, producing judicialized administration. If they cannot learn to have a greater understanding of what administration requires for success, it would be preferable to fire the more extreme of these two types and start all over again. In a national crisis, this would have to be done anyway.

There are too many specialists and too few generalists. The United States produces too many lawyers. One consequence of this is that the surplus try to make a living by working in the government or by representing interests that try to neutralize its efforts. There should be fewer lawyers, and better ones. Equally, public administration should be training fewer specialists and more potential general managers and chief executives. In both cases the reason for concentrating on the training of specialists is that technical subjects sound more scientific and more prestigious than philosophical, ethical, and historical-cultural things. Human material is taken that is broad to begin with and converted into cogs in a big machine that exacerbates the very excesses of bureaucracy that need to be altered. The more technical the country becomes, the more bureaucratic it becomes; the more bureaucratic it becomes, the larger becomes the number of specialists required to do the job that fewer specialists with skilled leadership could do better.

There are several ways this could be handled. The most encouraging would be for the leaders of the bar to face up to the issue fearlessly and patriotically. A second would be for governments to put a temporary ban on hiring lawyers in such large numbers. A third would be to give the civil service a drastic overhaul and abolish the idea that specialists can do the work of program managers simply because they have collected a lot of degrees. The fourth, which I shall deal with later, is to take a new look at the way lawyers and administrators are trained. The key to this is suggested by a headline in the New York *Times Book Review* of April 30, 1978: "Law Schools and Public-Law Schools." There is a need to create public law schools alongside the existing private law schools, or (what I think would be better policy) for existing schools to do a better job of preparing lawyers for statesmanship in government and public life generally. As the author of the *Times* article says, "Most graduates have not examined critically the economic and political premises of the legal institutions they will control; they have not learned how these institutions operate in society; nor have they reflected systematically on their roles and responsibilities as lawyers."

This lack of breadth and understanding may be accounted one of the main reasons that so many young lawyers, who should know better, have fallen in with the recent idea that judicializing administration is a cause comparable to seeking the Holy Grail. Not knowing what administration is, they do not know what they are doing to it. They like to feel superior and have learned in law school that law is rules, and hence they try to save the infidels in Washington by forcing their religion on them. The public administrators do not like what is going on, but they do not squawk very loudly because many of them are civil service legalists in their own way. The only ones who do complain are the outnumbered program managers, and many of them take higher paying jobs in industry or in the universities.

No country can thrive without a competent higher cadre of career executives serving the government. Some of the reasons for this are: they provide continuity of leadership and expertise in a country where continuity is lacking; they are about as objective and as free from conflict of interest as any body of skilled individuals a representative government is likely to find; they have the skills needed to stop the draining of the country's resources on nonprofitable ventures; they are principled enough to handle sublegislation and administrative decision making in an acceptable manner, because essentially their traits are similar to those of the best judges in our system; they are incorruptible and so can stop the loss of popular support for all government; and they are essentially middle-of-the-road politically, and hence no threat to private enterprise. It is a mistake to tie the hands of this group because they are the principal support for continuing free institutions in the United States. To confirm this conclusion, one need only see how countries such as Sweden, France, or Switzerland use such men to advantage.

The Administrative Procedure Act ought to be abrogated in favor of a program-by-program approach to assuring administrative justice. A team of top-flight lawyers and public administrators should make the study that is needed to do this. They should be equal in number in order to effect the needed reconciliation between the two competences. The job would not be as difficult as it sounds. They should discard the term "administrative procedure" in favor of the simpler term, "administration." They would consider the substantive and the so-called adjective law together, as always should be done. (Something can be learned from the Soviets here. They have close to 2,000 institutes training future leaders in all fields, and in all or most of them, they teach management; the management grows out of the subject matter, and is not taught in splendid isolation.)

The real reason the American Bar Association was so upset in the first place has to do with a very small area of administration—the independent regulatory commissions and the National Labor Relations Board (this, perhaps more than anything else, because it represented a new threat to big business). Since this is true, the reexamination should be initially concentrated on this area. Perhaps the ultimate conclusion would be to abolish some of these commissions and find other solutions.

I have suggested in Chapter 8 how sublegislation could be improved: start with more initiative on the part of career executives; use experienced administrators to draft legislation in the legislative branch; do away with all the formalism and time-consuming tactics of hearings on rules and let administrators handle this their own way, which is a better way; talk about policies and standards and drop the nondescriptive phrase rule making; step up training programs in action agencies in order to give officials at all levels a clear idea of how substance and organization interact and what they need to do to improve fairness; make use of administrative audits—or the kinds of outside checks that Walter Gellhorn writes about in all his books—to make sure that from the citizen's standpoint the administrators are doing a good job; finally, train all future administrators in the elements of law, and especially administrative law, as I hope it will be taught in the future.

As for administrative adjudication, the stultifying idea of having a semiautonomous judiciary inside the walls of administration should be forgotten. Let the chief administrator handle decisions of all kinds that come under his unified jurisdiction and control. As I suggested in my Immigration illustration, check to make sure that administrative reviews within the same department or agency are fair and handled by officials other than those who made the initial decision. Take extra precautions to see that parties seeking additional relief have exhausted all their administrative remedies before constitutional courts will agree to take jurisdiction. Do everything possible to reduce the overload on the regular court system.

Then take all the various special courts (like tax appeals) that have been created in recent years, and those that are about to be created, and organize them like the French and others do their administrative courts. The American Bar Association gave serious thought to this solution at one time, and it is unfortunate that they abandoned it. It would have been a much better solution than passing the Administrative Procedure Act of 1946. I grant that our hearing examiners and administrative law judges often do a good job, but they would be even brighter ornaments if they were outside of the departments and agencies and in a court system of their own. They would have nothing to do with internal administration. Instead, their function would be confined to appeals cases or to ones that have to do with conflict of interest, bias, excess of power, or some other ground that administrative courts handle on the Continent. Such an arrangement would take some of the load off constitutional courts without threatening their essential responsibilities.

The rule of law, which is the great ideal lying beyond Anglo-American concepts of due process, does not necessarily mean that a single court or type of court should decide all cases arising in the country. Administrative courts would be similar to other specialized courts, such as tax courts and the court of claims. Like all courts in the nation, this one too would head up to the U.S. Supreme Court.

The case for greater discretion rests upon the need to produce an improved and energetic administration of the laws. Just as one sets priorities by choosing among alternatives, so in the unfolding of a given program one chooses constantly between possible alternatives. Some of these have to do with substance, some with method, the most important ones with both. No administrator is worthy of the name unless he is adequately trained in both. There is such a thing as transferability of skills, enabling the same individual to succeed in areas as disparate as banking and agriculture, but anyone with common sense knows that it takes at least two years to learn to do either. Methods come out of substance, not vice versa.

In short, what I want to see happen is this: restore the program manager to his former position of confidence and respect, in which he was given sufficient autonomy and discretion to be a real leader. At the same time, confine the role of the lawyer in government to giving advice, as any good departmental solicitor would. If lawyers want to become administrators, let them shift gears and change their personalities so that they become hard-hitting production people. Many are capable of this, but only after going through a necessary metamorphosis. Then let the bar associations stop playing power politics and instead encourage their members to serve on citizen boards and commissions that seek better ways of organizing and running the government.

Turning now to curricular reform, it should be recognized at the outset that this is no easy undertaking. As explained in Chapter 7 from approximately 1880 until 1940, teachers of administrative law and government were one great fraternity. Some prestigious institutions, such as Columbia University, still carry on this tradition and call their department of government, "public law and jurisprudence," which seems to me a fortunate circumstance. Walter Gellhorn has throughout his professional career, commencing in the 1930s, kept one foot in this department and the other in the law school. Similarly, Nathaniel L. Nathanson of Northwestern Law School has been steadfastly interested in binding the two disciplines together; consult, for example, his article in the *American Political Science Review* (vol. 45, 1951) entitled "Central Issues of American Administrative Law," or his reaction to the Administrative Procedure Act in *Illinois Law Review* (vol. 41, 1947). But generally, throughout the country the two fields of law and administration have at best a quiet tolerance toward each other, and in some institutions it represents a downright antipathy.

Why did most law schools drop their political science orientation? Partly because the law curriculum became so vast and complex that they had to retrench in order to go deep. Even in the case of administrative law, which in recent years has been taught in all 105 law schools (the number is doubtless larger at this writing), and even though administrative law is one of the most popular courses in the curriculum, it has been found necessary in most cases to restrict the focus to regulation, the administrative tribunals, and the protection of private rights when dealing with the government. When this is done rigorously, as in Stason's casebook *The Law of Administrative Tribunals* (1947), an academically respectable and manageable focus is clearly effected.

When the course is limited, the inevitable consequence is to neglect the teaching of political systems, political philosophy, and public policy, resulting in the turning out of practitioners and future law professors and judges who are narrow in their outlook and understanding. I recall having several in-depth conversations with Leon Green, who was then dean of the law school at Northwestern University in the 1940s. He proposed that Corwin Edwards, an economist, and I teach a first-year course in the law school on the interconnections between economics and government, in which we would stress organization, philosophy, and public policy. Yale Law School began this emphasis even earlier and has made a marked success of it. Generally it is costly and difficult to pry loose professors in related fields such as economics, political science, and sociology, and get them to devote sufficient time and attention to the law school curriculum. They lose standing in their original professional field when this happens.

In the case of professional curricula in public administration, which have multiplied rapidly since the 1940s, the explanations of narrow inbreeding are understandably similar. The tendency has been for schools of public administration to proliferate, so that now there are almost as many of these programs as there are law schools, with more being created every year. They give special degrees, such as the M.A. and Ph.D. in public administration, rather than in political science. As this has occurred, the original departments of political science tend to give less attention, rather than more, to the fields of public administration and public law. In both areas, public law is now less emphasized than it was 40 years ago. The emphasis has shifted away from law and jurisprudence as the core of government studies, to government as the distributor of values, benefits, and rewards, in which pressure groups and public opinion, centering on politics, have become the chief focus. The result is that almost two generations of graduates in political science and public administration have emerged who know little about jurisprudence and administrative law (though more about constitutional law).

The third development that is significant for understanding the problem is that in even more recent days the tendency has been to create professional schools where management is taught generically, combining private and governmental management and administration, with attention to public policy but little or no formal course work in law and jurisprudence. Examples are the Harvard Business School, the School of Comparative Management at Cornell University, and more recently the well-financed comparative management professional schools at Northwestern and Yale Universities. With all its merits, this development tends to accentuate management as a skill, not a substantive field, in a manner strikingly similar to the law schools' focus on procedure as the whole of administrative law, with its resulting skewing of what administration is about and its neglect of the larger purposes of political economy it should be serving.

Early in their careers, whether in law, comparative management, or public administration, students should be introduced to the importance of administration and public policy in the life of the nation. A few good books would suffice. I think of a book such as Charles Lindblom's *Politics and Markets* (1977), written by a Yale economist turned political scientist. Equally effective would be Emmette Redford's *Democracy in the Administrative State* (1969) or Dwight Waldo's *The Study of Public Administration* (1955). From the law school offering there is a growing range of choice, as represented by William Cary's *Politics and the Regulatory Agencies* (1967), H. J. Friendly's *The Federal Administrative Agencies* (1962), Walter Gellhorn's *Federal Administrative Proceedings* (1941), or the recent article by Cutler and Johnson in *Yale Law Review* (1975), "Regulation and the Political Process."

In order to get the feel of administration as a unified operation early in their careers, law school students should be encouraged to read any one of a number of works mentioned in earlier chapters of this book, such as the one by Drucker. Or, if a shorter treatment is all that is possible, one might consult the present author's ruminations on 50 years of research in an article called "Revitalized Program Management," *Public Administration Review* (1978). The important thing is to whet the budding lawyer's appetite early in his career, with the result that some of the more promising of them (who will enter public life or become professors or judges) will develop a philosophical interest that will expand and become a constant in later life. I doubt the feasibility of teaching the combined course on economics and political science that Leon Green favored, but if that were possible I would strongly endorse it.

Early in U.S. development, economics came from the same unified source as law, political science, sociology, and history. Hence it is not surprising that for a considerable period, as exemplified by John R. Commons's work at Wisconsin, economists were in the thick of the public law offering—and some still are. I think it quite likely, as J. Kenneth Galbraith suggested in his presidential address to the American Economic Association, or as he more fully developed the thought in *The New Industrial State* (1967), that out of sheer necessity economics and political science will draw together again in the near future. This will happen because economists are weak on institutions and management, and political scientists are weak on the market system and its bearing on public policy. Law, economics, and political science make an ideal combination, and it was that vision that Hohfeld, Llewellyn, Hamilton, and others had at Yale Law School.

What do future public administrators need to know about law, and especially administrative law? They should be required to read books such as Roscoe Pound's *An Introduction to the Philosophy of Law* (1922, 1954), Bernard Schwartz's *The Law in American Life: A History* (1974), John Rawls's *A Theory of Justice* (1974), or Robert Summers's *Essays in Legal Philosophy* (1968, 1976). The reading of a book such as Pound's tends to settle the mind and give one a judicious outlook on life that administrators very much need. In the 1930s and 1940s I made an interview study of the leaders of the United States' largest corporations, and the ones I still remember that imparted the most wisdom are those who had judicial temperaments: Owen D. Young, Walter Gifford, Bancroft Gherardi, Alfred P. Sloan, and Arthur Page, to mention only a few. When looking for a good chief executive, look for the traits that make top-flight judges revered in history.

A course on administrative law should be taught wherever

managers are being trained: in political science, schools of public administration, business schools, and schools such as Yale, Northwestern, and Cornell where the emphasis is comparative. The writings of J. Roland Pennock, beginning with his treatise, *Administration and the Rule of Law* (1941), and coming down through his textbook on U.S. government, are particularly recommended. It is a pity that he has not been more widely recognized by law school teachers and writers. Similarly, wide use should be made of all the books written by Walter Gellhorn.

Unfortunately, there is no casebook in existence today that fills the bill for courses of this kind, but I predict that one soon will be written, possibly by one of the younger law school professors who is turning again to his political science antecedents. James Hart's "Introduction" (pp. 3–30) is a must in his *An Introduction to Administrative Law* (1950). This book is important as the only fairly recent treatment of the subject by a political scientist. Other things in Hart's book also should be read, but need not be gone into deeply, such as his "Extraordinary Legal Remedies," with which he begins his treatment. I doubt whether his Part II, "Public Office and Public Officers," needs intensive attention, because the same material can be better taught in a good course on personnel administration (unfortunately, that is rarely done today). Part III on "The Personal Liability of Officers," though increasingly timely, need not be studied in detail. Part V, called "Administrative Procedure," is covered more adequately in a basic course on business management or public administration. Everything else in this book deserves careful study.

What then is the basic substance of administrative law that should be taught to future managers? I advise not attempting to cover too much ground intensively, for it would be plainly eclectic and might prove superficial. Instead, after the background reading suggested above, the concentration should be on the problem areas dealt with in Part II of this present book: the making of law, sublegislation, administrative adjudication, and discretion. The problems of judicial review and of democratic control and responsibility also should be reemphasized.

In general, if public administration and law school administrative law are to form a companionable marriage, the guiding principle should be for each to stress, more than it has in recent years, the areas in which it has been weak in comparison with the other. But the core could be the same for both.

Method of instruction is important because one of the reasons that administrative law as taught in law schools has become too limited is that too much time is spent on cases. There ought to be more lecturing, because this makes it possible to cover a larger area of things that are important and enables the student to see the entire terrain. Similarly, more credit should be given for independent reading—even browsing—because habits established at this time are likely to continue into professional life. These observations apply quite as much to nonlaw school courses as to those given in schools of law themselves. Good teaching in law schools is rigorous, tough, and demanding, and the case method is an ideal vehicle for this purpose. But like any good thing, it can be overdone. The country needs lawyers who will be self-taught throughout life. Some of them seem never to crack a book again once they start to practice.

I also favor having individuals in both professions share, if only temporarily, the milieu of the other. No future professor of administrative law should be allowed to teach his subject long until he has equipped himself with at least two years of administrative experience in government. One of the ways of doing this is to take advantage of the excellent internship programs that are now available for White House, departmental, congressional, and judicial fellow residencies. Similarly, the candidate in management is well advised to steal a leaf from the experience of the law student and enroll in a law class, for at least one semester, after he takes his first job in the government. The best way for lawyers and administrators to communicate with each other is to clip the horns of their divisive mental sets. Even a short experience in each of the two fields tends to dispel the otherwise inherent prejudice quickly.

One of the fruitful ways by means of which differences in viewpoint and mental set between the legal and administrative professions may be reconciled, is by a patient perusal of each other's case materials. The long, tedious, sometimes abstruse decisions of law courts are often unattractive to the nonlegal student for at least two reasons: the decisions are not conveniently at hand, and they often make use of terms concerning which he has little understanding. However, if students of administration are exposed to a few cases, these fears are usually overcome. Thereafter the student is able to read decisions of the Supreme Court or other review tribunals with little difficulty. This developing self-confidence is facilitated, if, as is now often possible, he is able to relate the words of a decision to a situation in real life with which he already has some familiarity. This may be called the cross-referencing of administrative and judicial case materials.

The Inter-University Case Program in Public Administration and Policy Development, which commenced in 1948, has published more than 150 accounts of actual administrative situations. This program, supported by several universities and foundations, provides some excellent studies for cross-referencing with law. The first book-length volume, edited by Harold Stein and called *Public Administration and Policy Development: A Case Book* (1952), deals with a number of main subdivisions in public administration, such as organization, personnel, and control, but the main emphasis of the leading cases is on institutional decision making. It is because of this that the law student soon gets, in simulated fashion to be sure, the feel of administrative situations. As a minimum, every law student should read Stein's 14-page "Introduction," in which he not only deals with the nature and history of this field of public administration, but also writes knowingly on the merits and shortcomings of the case method itself.

Some of the longer and more interesting cases dealing with program management, and especially public policy and decision making, are these: *The Reconversion Controversy, The Defense Plant Corporation, The Disposal of the Aluminum Plants, The TVA Ammonia Plant, The Sale of the Tankers*, and *The King's River Program*. Many equally interesting and worthwhile cases have appeared since, but I shall not try to go into them. (The headquarters of the Inter-University Case Program is now at Syracuse University.)

There are a number of well-known administrative law cases that might be read in conjunction with this central focus on program development. On the subject of delegation of power, sublegislation, and rule making, there is *Yakus* v. *United States* (321 U.S. 414 [1944]), having to do with the Emergency Price Control Act of 1942; *United States* v. *Curtiss-Wright Export* (299 U.S. 304 [1936]), a controversial case pertaining to the so-called inherent powers of the president. Equally notable cases are *Buttfield* v. *Stranahan* (192 U.S. 470 [1904]); *Prentis* v. *Atlantic Coast Line Co.* (211 U.S. 210 [1908]); or *F.C.C.* v. *RCA Communications, Inc.* (346 U.S. 86 [1953]), one of the Frankfurter decisions.

On the subject of judicial review of regulatory decisions and the consideration to be given to administrative expertise, the turning point in the law, following a number of cases such as *Munn* v. *Illinois* and *Smyth* v. *Ames*, was *F.P.C.* v. *Hope Natural Gas Co.* (320 U.S. 591 [1944]), which cheered a number of administrators and increased their discretion. Also on the subject of discretion was *Lichter* v. *United States* (334 U.S. 742[1948]), which had to do with the Renegotiation Act passed at the end of World War II. *Chicago & So. Airlines* v. *Waterman S. Corp.*, dealing with overseas airline routes, throws light on the president's discretionary powers. *Reetz* v. *Michigan* (188 U.S. 505 [1903]) deals with the licensing of physicians in Michigan.

Other cases that I have chosen because of their similarity to real life situations that administrators are used to, are these dealing with the directing powers of administrators: *NLRB* v. *Jones & Laughlin Steel Co.* (301 U.S. 1 [1937]); an oft-cited case, *FTC* v. *Morton Salt Co.*, (334 U.S. 37 [1948]); *FTC* v. *Cement Institute* (333 U.S. 683 [1948]); *American Power Co.* v. *SEC* (329 U.S. 90 [1946]); and a case that caused almost as much of a stir as the *Morgan* case, and went to the Supreme Court twice, *SEC* v. *Chenery Corp.* (318 U.S. 80 [1943] and 332 U.S. 194 [1947]). All of the cases referred to in this paragraph can be found in Hart's 1950 casebook on administrative law.

Good cases on the due process of law requirements of notice and hearing are these: *ICC* v. *L&N R.R.* (227 U.S. 88 [1913]); *Ohio Bell Tel. Co.* v. *Public Util. Comm.* (301 U.S. 292 [1937]); and the *Cement Institute* decision referred to above.

On the relations between examiners and their agencies, see *Riss & Co.* v. *United States* (341 U.S. 907 [1951]), and *Universal Camera Corp.* v. *NLRB* (340 U.S. 474 [1951]).[1]

I have cited enough Supreme Court decisions to illustrate how in areas such as policy formation, sublegislation, decision making, notice and hearing, and administrative finality there are possibilities of matching up leading cases in public administration and administrative law. It is similar to the method Frankfurter used in teaching his course at Harvard Law School: start with the controversy, study it in the administrative agency, and see what happens when the case gets to the courts. Insofar as this method is used with skill and by reaching out to connected issues, it is possibly the best teaching method that has ever been devised, especially if the students do a great deal of independent reading.

Both law and public administration are a bit different than some other professions. The medical doctor, for example, sees so many patients daily that he needs to develop a sixth sense: this is poison ivy, German measles, or something else. In the case of the lawyer/administrator, however, his principal stock-in-trade is good judgment and knowing where to get the information he needs. He cannot possibly carry around in his head everything he needs (nor can the physician, for that matter, and that is why he has laboratories). My point is that the best training for both lawyers and administrators is knowing the principles, having a disciplined way of digging out the relevant information, and demonstrating good judgment in using one's own time and the time of others. This argues for fewer courses, fewer cases, and more independent digging. Ideally, academic training should be combined with experience on the job.

Administrators do not believe that administrative law could or should be depoliticized and made merely aseptic. The challenge of being an administrator is to equate one's role with statesmanship, not to play the part of a eunuch. With the introduction of the Administrative Procedure Act, the professional public administrator was increasingly alienated from the legal profession. His challenge was in assuming that he helped to mold and defend the country by dealing with policy and objectives, as the lawmaker does, and by using his acumen to get things accomplished, as the businessman does. Instead, the lawyers seemed to be telling him that substance is none of his business and that discretion is a bad thing because everything in automated administration ought to be reduced to rote. It was the image of the mechanical man that caused the revolt. "Their's but to do or die" was not regarded as a suitable slogan to be put on the wall of the government executive.

During the course of the past 40 years I have many times speculated on the reasons why political scientists reacted so emotionally when Charles A. Beard uttered his famous imprecation against "the tyranny of the lawyer." Was the mass exodus from public law due to a desire to find something more realistic? This was often said, and the new discovery was pressure groups. Or was it because lawyers had earned a reputation for conservatism, and the New Deal period was unsympathetic to that mood? Or was it because political scientists chose other emphases that were less demanding than legal scholarship? Perhaps we shall never know, but if we do, it is unlikely that any single explanation is the real one.

It is now time that law should be seen as more attractive than it has long been regarded. Lawyers are not parasites or merely hatchetmen for "the malefactors of great wealth." In any fair view of the situation, their collective role is as constructive and culturally significant as that of the government executive, whose altruism often is very great.

With a minimum of sentimentality and a maximum of realism, I submit that lawyers and administrators ought to stand together in what I think will be difficult years ahead. Public law ought to be recognized as a distinct and much admired field in the organization of codes, law schools, and arts and sciences courses in political science and public administration. In the troublous period ahead, there is a far greater danger in neglecting public law than in assuming (with little justification in fact) that its recognition disposes one to look reverentially on the all-powerful political state. I suggest taming the animal with understanding and cooperation, not ostracism and contempt.

NOTE

1. In the Inter-University Case Program series, see William H. Riker, *The National Labor Relations Field Examiner* (1951), and W. M. Fisk, *Administrative Procedure in a Regulatory Agency* (1965).

SELECTED BIBLIOGRAPHY

In drawing up a list of books and articles that might prove useful and provocative to anyone wishing to explore one or both fields, I have been influenced by the following considerations: there are certain books and articles that I have found invaluable in teaching administrative law and public administration; second, I have not thought it necessary to mention all the books and articles found in the notes, but only some of them; and third, I have tried to pick books and articles that relate to the philosophy and teaching of the two fields, because this nexus has some rich rewards for those who wish to explore it.

"Administrative Discretion." *Law and Contemporary Problems* 37 (Winter 1972).

Administrative Law Process: Better Management is Needed. Report of the Comptroller General of the United States to Congress. Washington, D.C., May 15, 1978.

Administrative Procedure Act: Legislative History. Sen. Doc. No. 248, 79th Cong., 2d sess. (1946).

Administrative Procedure in Government Agencies: Final Report of Attorney General's Committee on Administrative Procedure. Sen. Doc. No. 8, 77th Cong., 1st sess. (1941).

Arnold, Thurman. "The Role of Substantive Law and Procedure in the Legal Process." *Harvard Law Review* 45 (1932): 617–47.

Azreal, Jeremy R. *Managerial Power and Soviet Politics.* Cambridge: Harvard University Press, 1966.

Barnard, Chester. *The Functions of the Executive.* Cambridge: Harvard Business School, 1938.

Benjamin, Robert M. *Administrative Adjudication in the State of New York.* 6 vols. Albany, 1942.

Berle, A. A., Jr. "The Expansion of American Administrative Law.", *Harvard Law Review* 30 (March 1917): 430–48.

Bickel, Alexander. *The Morality of Consent.* New Haven: Yale University Press, 1975.

Blachly, Frederick E., and Oatman, Miriam E. *Federal Regulatory Action and Control.* Washington, D.C.: The Brookings Institution, 1940.

Burger, Warren E. *Agenda for 2000 A.D.—A Need for Systematic Anticipation.* The Pound Conference at St. Paul, April 7–9, 1976.

———. *Annual Report on the State of the Judiciary*. American Bar Association, midwinter meeting, Chicago, Illinois, February 23, 1976.

Cannon, Mark W. "Administrative Change and the Supreme Court." *Judicature* 57 (March 1974): 334–41.

Chamberlain, Joseph P., et al. *The Judicial Function in Federal Administrative Agencies*. New York: Columbia University Press, 1942.

Cohen, Morris R. *Law and the Social Order: Essays in Legal Philosophy*. New York: Harcourt, Brace & Co., 1933.

Comer, J. P. *Legislative Functions of National Administrative Authorities*. New York: Columbia University Press, 1927.

Committee on Ministers' Powers, Great Britain. *Minutes of Evidence and Report*. Cmd 4,060.

Cooper, Frank E. *State Administrative Law*. Indianapolis: Bobbs-Merrill, 1965.

Cooper, Robert M. "The Proposed United States Administrative Court." *Michigan Law Review* 25 (1937): 193–252, 565–96.

Cutler, Lloyd N., and Johnson, David R. "Regulation and the Political Process." *Yale Law Journal* 84 (1975): 1,395.

Davis, Kenneth C. *Discretionary Justice: A Preliminary Inquiry*. Baton Rouge: Louisiana State University Press, 1969.

———. *Administrative Law and Government*. St. Paul: West Publishing, 1960.

———. *Administrative Law Treatise*. 4 vols. St. Paul: West Publishing, 1958.

———. *Administrative Law*. St. Paul: West Publishing, 1951.

———. "Separation of Functions in Administrative Agencies." *Harvard Law Review* 61 (March 1948): 612–55.

Davis, Kenneth C. and European Associates. *Discretionary Justice in Europe and America*. Urbana: University of Illinois Press, 1976.

Davison, J. Forrester, and Grundstein, Nathan D. *Administrative Law and the Regulatory System*. Washington, D.C.: Lerner Law Book, 1968.

Dicey, Albert V. "The Development of Administrative Law in England. *Law Quarterly Review* 31 (1915): 148–53.

Dimock, Marshall E. "Revitalized Program Management." *Public Administration Review* 38 (May–June 1978): 199–204.

———. *Administrative Vitality: The Conflict with Bureaucracy*. New York: Harper & Row, 1959.

———. *The Executive in Action*. New York: Harper & Row, 1945.

———. "Forms of Control over Administrative Action." In *Essays on the Law and Practice of Governmental Administration*, edited by C. G. Haines and M. E. Dimock. Baltimore: Johns Hopkins University Press, 1935.

———. "The Role of Discretion in Modern Administration." In John M. Gaus et al., *The Frontiers of Public Administration*. Chicago: University of Chicago Press, 1936.

———. "Some Aspects of American Administrative Law." *Public Administration* (London) 9 (October 1931): 417–22.

Dimock, Marshall E. and Dimock, G. O. *Public Administration*. 4th ed. New York: Holt, Rinehart & Winston, 1969.

Drucker, Peter F. *Management: Tasks, Responsibilities, Practices*. New York: Harper & Row, 1973.

Dworkin, Ronald. *Taking Rights Seriously*. Cambridge: Harvard University Press, 1977.

Fairlie, John A. "Public Administration and Administrative Law." In *Essays on the Law and Practice of Governmental Administration*, edited by C. G. Haines and M. E. Dimock. Baltimore: Johns Hopkins University Press, 1935.

Field, Oliver P. *Some Suggested Research Projects in Administrative Law*. New York: Social Science Research Council, 1937.

Frankfurter, Felix. "The Task of Administrative Law." *University of Pennsylvania Law Review*, 75 (May 1927): 614–21.

Freeman, Harrop A. "Administrative Law in the First-Year Curriculum." *Journal of Legal Education* 10 (1957): 225–31.

Freund, Ernst. "The Law Back of Public Management." *Public Management* 14 (February, 1932): 57-60.

——. *Legislative Regulation*. New York: Commonwealth Fund, 1932.

——. "Historical Survey." In *The Growth of American Administrative Law*, edited by John A. Kurz and Charles Nagel. St. Louis: Thomas Law Book, 1923.

——. *Legislative Regulation*. New York: Commonwealth Fund, 1932.

——. "The Substitution of Rule for Discretion in Public Law." *American Political Science Review* 9 (November 1915): 666–76.

Fuchs, Ralph F. "The Hearing Examiner Fiasco under the Administrative Procedure Act." *Harvard Law Review* 63 (March 1951): 737–68.

——. "Concepts and Policies in Anglo-American Administrative Law Theory." *Yale Law Journal* 47 (February 1938): 538–76.

Fuller, Lon. *Anatomy of the Law*. New York: Praeger, 1968.

——. *The Morality of Law*. New Haven: Yale University Press, 1964.

Galloway, George B. *The Legislative Process in Congress*. New York: Thomas Y. Crowell, 1953.

Gellhorn, Ernest, and Robinson, Glen O. "Perspectives on Administrative Law." *Columbia Law Review* 75 (1975): 771.

Gellhorn, Walter. *Federal Administrative Proceedings*. Baltimore: Johns Hopkins University Press, 1941.

——. *Administrative Law: Cases and Comments*. Chicago: Foundation Press, 1940.

Goodnow, Frank J. *The Principles of the Administrative Law of the United States*. New York: Putnam's, 1905.

——. *Comparative Administrative Law*. 2 vols. New York: Putnam's, 1893.

Green, Mark. *The Other Government: The Unseen Power of Washington Lawyers*. New York: Grossman, 1975.

Griffith, J.A.G., and Street, Harry. *Principles of Administrative Law*. 2d ed. London: Pitman, 1957.

Gulick, Luther H., and Urwick, L. *Papers on the Science of Administration*. New York: Institute of Public Administration, 1937.

Haines, Charles Grove. "The Adaptation of Administrative Law and Procedure to Constitutional Theories and Principles." *American Political Science Review* 34 (1940).

Hart, H. L. A. *The Concept of Law*. Oxford: Clarendon Press, 1961.

Hart, James. *An Introduction to Administrative Law*. 2d ed. New York: Appleton-Century-Crofts, 1950.

Hayek, F. A. *Law, Legislation, and Liberty*. 2 vols. Chicago: University of Chicago Press, 1973.

Heady, Ferrel. *Administrative Procedure Legislation in the States*. Ann Arbor: University of Michigan, 1952.

Hyneman, Charles S. "Administrative Adjudication: An Analysis." *Political Science Quarterly* 51 (September 1936): 383–417.

Jackson, Robert H. *The Struggle for Judicial Supremacy*. New York: Knopf, 1941.

Jaffe, Louis L. *Judicial Control of Administrative Action*. Boston: Little, Brown, 1965.

———. "The Report of the Attorney General's Committee on Administrative Procedure." *University of Chicago Law Review* 8 (April 1941): 401–40.

Jowell, Jeffery L. *Law and Bureaucracy: Administrative Discretion and the Limits of Legal Action*. Port Washington, N.Y.: Dunellen Publishing, 1975.

Katz, Milton. *Cases and Materials on Administrative Laws*. St. Paul: West Publishing, 1947.

Kohlmeier, Louis, Jr. *The Regulators*. New York: Harper & Row, 1969.

Kraines, Oscar. *The World and Ideas of Ernst Freund: The Search for General Principles of Legislation and Administrative Law*. University: University of Alabama Press, 1974.

Landis, James M. *The Administrative Process*. New Haven: Yale University Press, 1938.

Learned, E. P., Ulrich, D. N., and Booz, D. R. *Executive Action*. Cambridge: Harvard Business School, 1951.

Leiserson, Avery. *Administrative Regulation: A Study in Representation of Interests*. Chicago: University of Chicago Press, 1942.

Lieberman, Jethro K. *Crisis at the Bar: Lawyers' Unethical Ethics and What to Do About It*. New York: Norton, 1977.

Lindblom, Charles. *Politics and Markets*. New York: Basic Books, 1977.

Lorch, Robert S. *Democratic Process and Administrative Law*. Detroit: Wayne State University Press, 1969.

McGuire, O. R. "The Proposed United States Administrative Court." *American Bar Association Journal* 22 (1936): 197–202.

Moore, Wilbert. *The Professions: Roles and Rules*. New York: Russell Sage Foundation, 1970.

Musolf, Lloyd D. *Federal Examiners and the Conflict of Law and Administration*. Baltimore: Johns Hopkins University Press, 1953.

Nathanson, Nathaniel L. "The Growth of American Administrative Law." *American Political Science Review* 45 (June 1951): 348–85.

———. "Separation of Functions within Federal Administrative Agencies." *Illinois Law Review* 35 (April 1941): 901–37.

Nonet, Philippe. *Administrative Justice: Advocacy and Change in a Government Department*. New York: Russell Sage Foundation, 1969.

Parker, Reginald. "Why Do Administrative Agencies Exist?" *Georgetown Law Journal*. 45 (Spring 1957): 331–63.

Pennock, J. Roland. *Administration and the Rule of Law*. New York: Rinehart & Co., 1941.

Pennock, J. Roland and Chapman, John W. *Due Process*. New York: New York University Press, 1977.

———. *The Limits of Law. Nomos XV*. New York: Atherton, 1974.

Pound, Roscoe. *An Introduction to the Philosophy of Law*. New Haven: Yale University Press, 1922, 1954.

———. *Administrative Law: Its Growth, Procedure and Significance*. Pittsburgh, University of Pittsburgh, 1942.

———. *Contemporary Juristic Theory*. Claremont: Claremont Colleges, 1940.

President's Advisory Council on Executive Organization. *A New Regulatory Framework*. Washington, D.C.: Government Printing Office, 1971.

Reagan, Michael D., ed. "A Symposium: Are We Getting Anywhere?" *Public Administration Review*. 32 (July–August 1972): 283–310.

Redford, Emmette S. "Regulation Revisited." *Administrative Law Review* 28 (Summer 1976): 543–68.

———. *Democracy in the Administrative State*. New York: Oxford University Press, 1969.

———. *Administration of National Economic Control*. New York: Macmillan, 1952.

Robson, William A. *Justice and Administrative Law*. London: Macmillan, 1928.

Root, Elihu. "Public Service by the Bar." *American Bar Association Journal* 2 (July 1916): 736–55.

Rosenberry, Marvin B. "Administrative Law and the Constitution." *American Political Science Review* 23 (February 1929): 32–46.

Ruhlen, M. *Manual for Administrative Law Judges*. Washington, D.C., Administrative Conference of the United States, 1974.

Schleh, Edward C. *Management by Results*. New York: McGraw-Hill, 1961.

Schwartz, Bernard. *Administrative Law*. Boston: Little, Brown, 1976.

Schwartz, Bernard and Wade, H. W. R. *Legal Control of Government: Administrative Law in Britain and the United States*. Oxford: Clarendon Press, 1972.

Selznick, Phillip. *Law, Society, and Industrial Justice*. New York: Russell Sage Foundation, 1969.

———. *Leadership in Administration*. Evanston and White Plains: Row, Peterson, 1957.

Stason, E. Blythe. *The Law of Administrative Tribunals*. 2d ed. Chicago: Callaghan & Co., 1947.

Stewart, Robert B. "The Reformation of American Administrative Law. *Harvard Law Review* 88 (1975): 1,667.

Stone, Julius. *Social Dimensions of Law and Justice*. Stanford: Stanford University Press, 1966.

Summers, Robert S., ed. *Essays in Legal Philosophy*. Berkeley & Los Angeles:

University of California Press, 1976.

"A Symposium on Administrative Law, based upon Legal Writings, 1931–33." *Iowa Law Review* 18 (January 1933): 129–248.

Symposium on the Final Report of the Attorney General's Committee on Administrative Procedure, by Felix Frankfurter, A. H. Feller, John Foster Dulles, and J. Forrester Davison." *Columbia Law Review* 41 (April 1941): 585–645.

Symposium. "The Administrative Procedure Act." Articles by Roscoe Pound, Sylvester C. Smith, Jr., Hatton W. Summers, and others. *American Bar Association Journal* 30 (1940): passim.

Thomas, Rosamund. *The British Philosophy of Administration*. London & New York: Longman, 1978.

United States, Administrative Conference of. *Recommendations and Reports*. Vol. 1, 1968–70, serially.

Vanderbilt, Arthur T. "One Hundred Years of Administrative Law." In *Law: A Century of Progress* (1937), vol. 1, pp. 117–44.

Wade, H. W. R. *Administrative Law*. 2d ed. London: Oxford University Press, 1967.

Waldo, Dwight. *The Study of Public Administration*. New York: Doubleday, 1955.

———. *The Administrative State*. New York: Ronald Press, 1948.

Walker, Harvey. *Law Making in the United States*. New York: Ronald Press, 1934.

White, Leonard. *An Introduction to Public Administration*. New York: Macmillan, 1926.

Willoughby, W. F. *Principles of Legislative Organization and Administration*. Washington, D.C.: Brookings Institution, 1934.

———. *Principles of Judicial Administration*. Washington, D.C.: Brookings Institution, 1929.

———. *Principles of Public Administration*. Washington, D.C.: Brookings Institution, 1927.

Wilson, Woodrow. "The Study of Administration." *Political Science Quarterly* 2 (June 1887): 197–222.

Woll, Peter. "Administrative Law in the Seventies." *Public Administration Review* 32 (September-October 1972): 557–64.

Wollan, Laurin A., Jr. "Lawyers in Government." *Public Administration Review* 38 (March-April 1978): 105–12.

ABOUT THE AUTHOR

Marshall E. Dimock's principal academic connections have been at the University of Chicago, the University of California at Los Angeles, Northwestern University, and New York University. At NYU he was head of the All-University Department of Government. His main fields are business and government, public administration, and administrative law. He is the author of over 35 books and more than 200 articles.

Professor Dimock also has had extensive experience in government as a federal official, state legislator, and United Nations executive. His consulting activity in business and government goes back to 1932.

Professor Dimock received his A.B. degree from Pomona College and his Ph.D. Degree from Johns Hopkins University.